I Was There

**Residents of the
Clifford C. Sims State Veterans'
Nursing Home
Share Their Military Stories
with
Janet A. Nicolet**

10/13/12
To Chris,
Janet a. Nicolet

RealTime Publishing
Limerick, Ireland

Second Printing

Cover: The cover was designed by Kaitlyn Reiter and Elizabeth Cuthrell, students in the Digital Design Class at Haney Technical Center, Lynn Haven, Florida.

ISBN: 978-84961-096-4
Published by RealTime Publishing – Limerick, Ireland

Printed in the United States of America and Europe

Acknowledgements

- I am grateful to the staff at the Clifford C. Sims State Veterans' Nursing Home, who were so supportive throughout this journey, especially Virginia O'Hare, Activities Director.
- Mike Mancos, resident at Sims, went out of his way to assist me in this project.
- Editors Virginia Dixon, Wanda McGee, Janice Rench, Martha Spiva and Joyce Tarr, all gave so generously of their time and talent to edit this project in honor of the veterans.
- The families of the Sims' veterans have encouraged and helped in so many ways with their loved one's story.
- To my family and friends who have cheered me on during my writings.

Dedication

There are not enough words to express the appreciation to the military men and women of the United States who have served or are serving our country. Thank you for your devoted time and efforts in keeping our country safe. We are so proud of you!

Contents

Foreword

In *I Was There,* Janet Nicolet has turned back the clock and gathered the wartime remembrances of veterans at the Clifford C. Sims State Veterans' Nursing Home near Panama City, Florida.

Veterans of three wars tell their own stories, while Nicolet intertwines their unique first-hand experiences with reports from the home front to provide a fascinating perspective of the period.

From Pearl Harbor survivors to Medal of Honor recipients, her focus on those whose selfless service and sacrifice helped shape the latter half of the 20th Century is an inspiration to all.

R. Steven Murray
Communications Director
Florida Department of Veterans' Affairs

I Was There

**Clifford Chester Sims State Veterans' Nursing Home
near Panama City, Florida**

The moment you step through the door of the Clifford C. Sims State Veterans' Home you feel welcomed. That first warm greeting comes from the receptionist on duty. But it doesn't stop there. That same unique attitude permeates throughout the Home. The staff loves what they are doing; taking care of the men and women who once served our country. It is their way of saying "thank you".

During their service time, many of the residents spent grueling days and weeks fighting to keep the enemies of the United States from invading our country. Their battle scars in body and mind are still visible. Others served proudly in support roles. Not one of them liked being called *a hero*.

Some have said, "I didn't do anything special. I just sat behind a desk." Or, "I just filled boxes with supplies." Those in support roles are among the unsung heroes of the military. Day after day they lent their hands and efforts to provide those men on the front lines with everything they

I Was There

needed; food, clothing, soap, fuel, auto parts, plane parts, ammunition and so on.

The mounds of paperwork produced by men and women in office positions enabled the troops to receive their pay and families to be notified of injuries or deaths. They also kept track of the status and position of personnel for information purposes for the commanders.

Others were at base camps in positions of mechanics where that kept planes in A-1 condition for safe flights by the pilots and their crew members. Trucks were inspected and repaired by men and women who knew what they were doing.

Many of the residents of Sims Veterans' Home were just fresh out of high school or basic training when they were handed orders to go into war time action; their minds and emotions now filled with fear and anxiety. But soon they would mature on the shores of Normandy, in the rice fields of Vietnam, on the snow covered hills of Korea or on a ship in German submarine invested waters.

Decades later they call to mind their experiences with pride. They remember facts, dates and their buddies by name, but choke-up when sharing details of their friends who died on the battlefield. Their stories are on the pages that follow.

They were there!

I Was There

Day of Infamy

War in the Pacific

For two decades after World War I, Japan experienced earthquakes (dozens in 1920) and other natural disasters which effected the country socially and economically.

Japan's Great Depression hit that country in the mid-1920s leaving industrial workers without jobs and others who lost their life savings. To make matters worse, crops were seriously reduced because of repeated drought and cold weather. The economics of the country took another nose-dive when the United States was plunged into its Great Depression in 1929, and the large quantities of silk generally purchased from the Japanese ceased.

Japan's citizens died by the thousands from malnutrition, influenza and tuberculosis – while others survived on tree bark and roots. The entire country was at her lowest ebb.

The prospects of war in the Pacific began with Japan's intentions to take over Southeast Asia. Japan knew it had to curtail any intervention by the United States and Great Britain, thus they attacked Pearl Harbor.

The Imperial Japanese Navy Admiral, Isoroku Yamamoto, initiated the Japanese surprise air attack on Pearl Harbor with their superior zero fighter planes. They flew in from the *north* over Oahu, knowing that the main U. S. naval flotilla was stationed in Pearl Harbor on the *south* side of the island. They could only believe that the U.S. Navy would not be contemplating any kind of attack

I Was There

from the north. As they approached the island, the Japanese navy hoped to catch the military off guard on this Sunday morning. Their principal mission - cripple the Pacific Fleet.

On December 7, 1941 at 07:55 (Hawaiian time) the Japanese launched the first of three waves of attack planes. A total of three hundred and sixty planes sank or severely damaged eighteen ships, including eight battleships, three light cruisers and three destroyers. One hundred sixty one U.S. Army and Navy planes were destroyed and seventy-one Army and thirty-one Navy planes seriously damaged. The Japanese had successfully accomplished their mission.

The casualties suffered by the U. S. Navy and Marine Corps came to a total of two-thousand eight-hundred ninety-six. The Army lost two hundred-twenty-eight and over five-hundred wounded. Civilian casualties numbered fifty-seven, and many more were seriously injured.

An hour and a half after the Japanese planes attacked the U.S. Pacific Fleet in Pearl Harbor Colonel Hideo Ohira of Japan's Imperial Headquarters read the Imperial Rescript of War to newsmen that war had been declared upon the United States and Great Britain:

> "We, by grace of heaven, Emperor of Japan seated on the Throne of a line unbroken for ages eternal, enjoin upon you, Our loyal and brave subjects. We hereby declare war on the United States of America and the British Empire.
>
> The hallowed spirits of Our Imperial Ancestors guarding Us from above, We rely upon the loyalty and courage of Our subjects in Our confident expectation that the task bequeathed by

I Was There

Our forefathers will be carried forward, and the sources of evil will be speedily eradicated."

Japan stayed united even though its citizens were starving and could not imagine the thought of another war. The country's military airmen begged to be used in the war as Kamikaze pilots – willing to die for their country.

The battle for the islands of the Pacific continued after Pearl Harbor. Next on Japan's list were the other islands of the Pacific: Midway, the Philippines, Iwo Jima, Okinawa, Kwajalein, Tarawa and Eniwetok. The bloodshed continued for almost four more years.

WAR in EUROPE

Germany Declares War

The governments of Japan, Germany and Italy signed a ten-year pact on September 27, 1940 called *Tripartite Pact*. It stated in six articles of the Pact that Japan recognizes and respects the leadership of Germany and Italy in the establishment of a new order in Europe. It further stated that Germany and Italy respected the leadership of Japan in the establishment of a new order in Greater Asia.

Therefore, on December 8, 1941, it was not aggression by the United States that began the war with Japan but just the opposite. Japan had dropped bombs on Pearl Harbor the day before forcing the United States to declare war against Japan.

Germany and Italy, as a partner with Japan in the *Tripartite Pact,* declares war against the United States on December 11, 1941 for what they saw as enemy aggression toward Japan.

I Was There

World War II Era

Stories

**World War II Memorial in
Washington, D.C.**

PFC W. C. Hinton

was there at the

Battle of the Bulge

79th Infantry (Cross of Lorraine)

W. C. Hinton was born in 1920 in the northern Mississippi town of Houlka - population today is just over seven hundred. He was drafted into the army in 1943 at age twenty-three along with his three brothers. They all served their country in different capacities, and they *all* four came home – alive.

Private Hinton loved his black wavy hair and when he was told it had to come off, he put up a real verbal fight. But, you know who won. He completed two weeks basic training at Camp Wheeler, Georgia. After graduating he was assigned as a rifleman with the 79th Infantry Division. Private Hinton, quite a frugal man, was okay with that position as it would pay him an additional ten dollars a month for being a good combat soldier.

I Was There

It was there at Camp Wheeler that this young married man struggled, believing that he would be seeing for the last time his wife Gladys and two daughters Alice and infant Patricia.

Hinton's job was that of a replacement soldier. The men called it "fill holes on the front line." He would replace anyone who had been wounded or killed. His unit's assignment was to move from town-to-town, house-to-house in hand-to-hand combat against the Germans.

In August 1944, the Allies rushed across France with amazing speed. But before they could cross the Rhine River, they would have to face a last-stand German onslaught. Germany was clearly losing the war which made them try even harder for success. On the Eastern front, the Soviet Red Army was closing in, while at the same time the bombing by the Allies was inflicting devastation on German cities.

The battle that Private Hinton was engaged in was fought on an eighty-mile front that ran from southern Belgium through the Ardennes, and down to Ettelbruck in the middle of Luxembourg. On a map, that area looked like a westward bulging shape, so named the Battle of the Bulge.

The young private saw war at its worst. Much of the battle was affected by the bitterly cold weather. The temperature was the coldest on record and casualties from exposure to the cold grew in large numbers. Heavy snowstorms became a real problem. Another factor was that the Germans attacked in white uniforms so as to blend in with the snow. Weapons froze, so men urinated on them to thaw them. Trucks had to be run every half hour to keep the oil in them from freezing.

The men couldn't pin-point where they were -- they just kept marching on; day-after-day and week-after-week. Dead bodies were everywhere. The death toll in each city was so great that men had to climb over bodies to get through the town. Hinton said he can still hear the cries of young children who were starved, afraid and alone. Most were in desperate need of medical care.

The persistent deep snow caused the men's wet boots to become unbearable to wear, a hurdle that caused them to hunt for a pair on a dead man that would fit. The Army had bypassed shipments of winter gear in favor of ammunition and gasoline. So the men piled on as much clothing as they could to try and withstand the frigid weather. Weary and cold the men marched on to one city after another eradicating Germans from the bombed out homes and shops.

I Was There

There were times when the men had to dig a fox hole at a moment's notice when enemy bullets came in their direction. They used their hands or whatever else was available to dig a hole big enough to hide in. They were often pinned down in those fox holes for some time by a barrage of enemy fire. The Americans launched their attacks under the cover of darkness, as in their dark uniforms they stood out as perfect targets against the snow in daylight hours.

Many men came down with heavy colds and pneumonia from prolonged exposure. Whenever they could, foot soldiers would stop, wolf down cold rations and warm coffee, and again plod forward through the deep snow to their next objective.

As the men continued to move forward toward the Rhine River, they soon learned the difference in the sound of planes overhead, distinguishing the enemy planes from those of the Allies. They had to listen carefully as the sounds of war was riveting all around them with tanks being bombed and planes being shot down out of the sky.

Army engineers carried mine detectors and cautiously probed the snowy roads just ahead of the foot soldiers. The Germans had laid tubes filled with TNT that set off mines for seven feet around it. The deep snow covered up those deadly weapons; therefore the mine detectors were of great value. Still they had to be vigilant with every step they took.

In December 1944, General Eisenhower met in Verdon with his top field commanders to devise a plan to halt the Germans. Lieutenant General Patton was a part of that meeting. It was decided that infantry units of other divisions would join the depleting number of troops in Patton's Third Army

PFC Hinton's unit joined forces with Lt. General George Patton's III Army to cross the Rhine. Hinton is purported to be the first American to cross it.

PFC Hinton spent one and a half years in Europe during that awful war. When it finally ended, he was sent back to the States on a Freedom Ship. The seas were so rough that he was deathly ill the entire journey to the shoreline of the United States. German U-boats became a continual problem for the ship, causing it to change course time after time.

He returned to his wife and daughters and to his old job in Houlka, Mississippi at the Delta Trouser Factory, where he pressed men's dress pants after they came off the assembly line.

W.C. went through a great transition when he laid down his rifle and picked up civilian life, once again. He no longer had to worry about the danger of every step he took, but it still would take some time for this young man to settle down into a regular daily routine.

When asked if he wore the trousers made at the Delta Trouser Factory, he said with a grin, "Sure did. I would take the seconds (those with imperfections), pay three dollars and then fix whatever was wrong with them. At one time I had fifty pairs of pants."

Hinton worked at the factory for the next twenty-seven years. Then Gladys and W.C. decided to move to Panama City and purchase a motel on Highway 98, which they called Hilton's Motel. They managed it together for ten

I Was There

years and then sold it, but continued to live in Panama City, where he took up brick laying.

In 2006, Mr. Hinton moved into the Sims Veterans' Home after breaking a hip. Just two years later his beloved Gladys passed away.

W. C. Hinton has two children, four grandchildren and five great-grandchildren. His daughter, Pat Commander resides in Panama City and is her father's care giver. A couple of times a week she picks him up from Sims and takes him to the family home – a real blessing for him.

I Was There

S/Sgt. Ronnie J. Everitt
was there in Pearl Harbor
December 7, 1941

August 2004 George W. Bush Rally - Panama City Marina
Pearl Harbor Survivors
Ronnie Everitt (left) & Chris Chrastina
leading *Pledge of Allegiance*

On June 4, 1941, Ronnie Everitt raised his hand to take the oath to defend the United States of America. Before leaving home his father had said, "Son, you know you'll be gone for five years." "No, sir." was his son's speedy reply, "I'm only goin' for a year." But, father knows best, as Ronnie Everitt returned home five years later.

Ronnie was born in 1919 in the small town of Graceville in the Panhandle of Florida. At age twenty-two he enlisted in the Army at Camp Blanding, Florida – southwest of Jacksonville.

I Was There

His mother, Martha, was a homemaker and his dad, Carson Everitt, a meat cutter in Ronnie's grandfather's Graceville meat market. Martha became literally ill when she heard that her son was leaving for the Army, but would be a real trooper, praying for God's protection over him throughout the five years of his military service. The two communicated on a regular basis through letters.

Everitt attended electrician school in San Diego for only a few weeks before being shipped to Honolulu aboard the U.S.N.S. Taft, a Navy troop ship. The ship hit an enormous storm while at sea, with many of the lifeboats being washed overboard. In the midst of the tempest, a muster was called to get a head count. That roll call revealed all survived the storm but three. There was no report of what happened to the missing men.

The men slept five deep in bunks that gave each man very little breathing room; Private Everitt occupied the third one down. The Taft took on so much sea water during the storm that it stood six inches deep on the floor where the men slept. The journey seemed like it would never end.

His first glimpse of Pearl Harbor was not what a tourist would see today – palm trees, beautiful beaches, a coastline of high rise hotels and bikini clad sunbathers. Instead, Everitt saw a stretch of beach, a mass of trees and one long dirt road. But, what made a real impression upon this new recruit was the awesome accumulation of naval ships of every size in the harbor. That was the U.S. Pacific Fleet.

The ship docked and Everitt's unit headed for Camp Coast on the south side of Pearl Harbor. His main duty with the Coast Artillery unit was to check each radar system around the island every four hours to make sure they were in working condition.

Men from his company also manned twelve inch and sixteen inch guns positioned to fire at enemy ships endeavoring to enter Pearl Harbor from the south. But the thought of ever seeing an enemy ship sail into that harbor seemed far-fetched.

One evening, when all was quiet in Pearl Harbor, the men in Private Everitt's unit were just coming out of the mess hall from having dinner when a truck sped by on the dirt road out in front. It had four or five small barrels in the bed of the truck that were filled with honey bees being transported from one place to another. The truck hit a hole in the road and tipped over spilling out the barrels. Even though the containers had a piece of material covering the top, the jar of hitting the ground burst them open and out came the bees.

An officer yelled, "Don't fight 'em", as the bees swarmed the men. Private Everitt climbed a tree and kept his head and arms hid in the leaves, thus protecting himself from bee stings. Several men did not adhere to the officer's command and ended up getting stung everywhere – ears, arms, and head. They spent weeks in the hospital. Disobedience had a high price to pay.

The peaceful atmosphere of the tropical island of Oahu greatly changed on December 7, 1941 at 07:55 (Hawaiian time), the date United States President Franklin D. Roosevelt said would live on in infamy. It was also a day that Private Everitt will never forget.

On that beautiful sunny morning Everitt had risen early and was feeling mighty satisfied having just returned from breakfast. He was sitting in the dayroom reading a magazine when the building began to shake. Looking over at the only other person in the room, he asked, "What's goin' on here?"

"Ah, don't pay no attention to that. It's just the marines on maneuvers," said the sergeant in a flippant manner. The sergeant waited about three seconds and then jumped to his feet. "No! This is Sunday and they don't have maneuvers on Sunday."

Both men ran to the front door and could immediately see the Japanese zeros dive bombing Hickam Field and now heading straight toward their building. They stood hypnotized for a moment until they heard a sergeant yell, "Get to a shelter, now."

The Japanese strafed their area and one of the bullets came in at an angle and obliterated the wide steps where Private Everitt was standing. He only received scratches and bruises from the pieces of cement that flew up – but he was dazed mighty frightened.

Just then trucks from the motor pool suddenly appeared and took the men to man the twelve inch guns. On the way the men could see billows of smoke rising from the many fires in the harbor. Everitt and the others in the truck experienced the sound of numerous explosions that took place as another wave of Japanese zeros dropped their bombs that shook the ground profusely.

Only those on the ships and on the shoreline who lived to tell the story could paint the devastating picture of horror that took place that day. The scene was one of dead bodies aboard ships and floating in the water, twisted metal,

I Was There

explosions one after another and fires raged out of control as ships sunk to the bottom or tipped to the side.

U.S.S. West Virginia in the foreground bombed by the Japanese

Just the day before, the U.S. aircraft carriers, *Lexington*, *Enterprise* and *Saratoga* had set sail from Pearl Harbor for maneuvers at sea. This previously scheduled operation ultimately saved the lives of hundreds of men and their absence surprised the Japanese.

In U.S. President Franklin D. Roosevelt's speech on December 8th to the members of the Senate and House of Representatives he asked for a declaration of war against Japan. It is a speech Private Everitt will never forget, especially the line that says, *With confidence in our armed forces, with the unbounding determination of our people, we will gain inevitable triumph. So help us God.* Those words -- *so help us God* continued to play over and over in Private Everitt's mind for quite some time, giving him a sense of peace in the midst of turmoil. He had been raised in church and had a steadfast trust in God.

To make matters worse for the United States, only four days later, on December 11, 1941, war on the United States was declared by Germany and Italy. Now, more men would be called upon to take a stand against the enemy on another continent.

The men on Oahu continued their surveillance of the skies for the next six weeks. They manned those twelve inch guns in four hour shifts – but saw nothing. An eerie quiet prevailed that caused such an uneasiness.

The week after the war started Private Everitt was sent to Pearl Harbor to radar school. The scene he observed in the harbor was unbelievable. *How could this have happened?* Ships partially sunk, one battleship had rolled on its side, smoke still rose from other ships that had been bombed and the stench in the air was appalling.

Fear of another horrific attack, and not knowing what lie ahead for him, one night Private Everitt sat down on his bunk and wrote to his longtime girlfriend, Ollie, telling her to find someone else as he didn't think he would make it back home.

Day and night the military and civilian alike peered into the skies over Oahu wondering when the next Japanese attack would take place. Those who tended radar sites were on their toes, so to speak, keeping a watchful eye for enemy aircraft.

All was fairly quiet for Everitt for the next few years. In 1944, he had become a Staff Sergeant and moved from Camp Coast to Pearl Harbor. His duty consisted of checking the radar at the five different sites on Oahu for function ability.

He was on Diamond Head on August 15, 1945, attending a radar site when he heard the news over the radio that the war with Japan had ended. He shut everything down and instead of driving the jeep down the main road back to his unit in Pearl Harbor he headed straight down the mountain. With a big grin on his face he shouted out loud, "I'm going home. I'm going home" as he bounced along on that bumpy ride. Thankfully, he made it down without incident -- his mother had to have been praying.

Arriving at his unit, he immediately requested to be busted to a private and sent home. He was told, "I'd like to do that too, Everitt, but we can't. We'll get to you soon."

"But, when?"

A month later, Sergeant Everitt was on his way home aboard a troop ship. During that month of waiting, he just hung around the barracks. Many of the military buildings had been demolished by the Japanese attack so they used the kitchens and other facilities in vacated homes of the rich that were adjacent to their barracks.

Everitt's fondest remembrance of that time is swimming in Doris Duke's swimming pool. Duke, the tobacco heiress and philanthropist had built a beautiful seasonal estate near Diamond Head in 1935. She called it Shangri La and to Staff Sergeant Everitt that pool area became a real oasis for him.

Upon returning to the States he boarded a bus to Chipley, Florida and then a taxi to his hometown of Graceville. He was now a mature man returning from war and still a respectful and considerate Christian man. His mother recounted to him months later that during the war someone had approached her in church saying, "War ruins men. My son came home and he's turned out to be a no-good."

I Was There

Mrs. Everitt's reply was emphatic, "Not my son." She was right. Ronnie Everitt followed his Christian principles while in the service and continues to live that life today at age ninety-two.

Upon his return to his hometown, he began repairing radios in the back room of a shoe shop in the small town of Graceville. For the average citizen, the radio was the only vehicle in those days that they depended upon for daily news, besides the local newspaper. Television would come later.

Mr. Everitt married Ollie, his school sweetheart after he returned home. In the next couple of decades they raised six beautiful daughters – Ellen, Janis, Linda, Cathy, Victoria and Jennifer - all still living nearby today. Ollie had told Ronnie before they married that she didn't want any sons. She had been raised with several brothers who were mean to her, so she only wanted girls. He still shakes his head today when he tells that story and says, "Those were mighty powerful words – 'cause they came true. We only had girls."

Ronnie Everitt is still an active man. Regularly attends church and also meets on the second Thursday of every month at the Rodeo Restaurant in Panama City for lunch with Pearl Harbor Survivors. Twenty-eight members of the original group have now dwindled to two.

A young Ronnie Everitt was there that fateful day in Pearl Harbor when America was viciously attacked by a foreign enemy. Thankfully, he survived to tell his story.

Ships Serviceman Lee E. Elwell, II
was there on the
U.S.S. Laramie (AO-16)
when it was torpedoed

U.S.S. Laramie

Lee Elwell, a native Alabamian, was born in Ensley in 1923. Just prior to his eighteenth birthday Lee and his girlfriend, Catherine, had just returned to the Elwell home from a day of horseback riding. Opening the front door he found his mother in tears. She looked up and managed to say, "They've bombed Pearl Harbor."

While in high school, Lee and two of his buddies had made a pact that no matter what, they would stick together should they ever decide to join the military. But, after hearing the devastating news of war, their pact fell apart - one joined the Army, another the Marines and Lee enlisted in the Navy in January 1941. He would later return to Alabama, but sadly, neither of his friends ever made it back home, alive.

I Was There

To take his oath and attend basic training he traveled to Chicago to the Great Lakes Training Center where the snow was up to his knee caps. This Alabama boy had never seen snow like that. A few weeks later, Elwell headed home on a seven day furlough to marry Catherine.

He returned to Chicago and at the conclusion of basic training, names were called out for those who would report to Boston, Massachusetts. Elwell's name was not called. The next set of names would serve on a submarine. He held his breath not wanting submarine duty as he was a tall individual, and thankfully his name was not called. Next, the names were called out for those who would report to the U.S.S. Laramie, an auxiliary oil tanker. Elwell heard his named called. At that moment, it was an okay assignment for him. But, when he reported for duty and looked up at that ship tied up at the dock, he shook his head and said out loud, "What've I got myself into?"

The Laramie, nicknamed 'Galloping Goose' carried one-hundred and twenty octane airplane fuel, barrels of oil and general cargo to include depth charges to be delivered to several military operations that stretched from South America to Greenland. The Laramie fueled all types of military ships docked at U.S. radar installations in Brazil, Aruba, Southern Caribbean, Greenland and Iceland.

The Laramie sailed in a convoy of escort ships. Those ships were there to protect tankers, supply and troop ships from enemy fire. In 1943, Elwell recalls the Laramie being hit by a hurricane that pushed them from South America to New York in three days - a trip that generally took a week. Some of the convoy ships were lost during that storm.

I Was There

Twice a year, she sailed into the North Atlantic to deliver supplies and fuel to military posts in Greenland, where military aircraft leaving the United States for Britain would refuel.

During those trips, the Laramie would come upon icebergs that measured as high as a building, with six times that height under the water. Sometimes the ice would be so thick it sealed the passageway, making it impassable. The ship's captain would have to call for a plane to bomb the ice to break it up.

Elwell and others who were on gun watch were on duty in four hour shifts. They wore heated suits with batteries in their boots. They were spelled by someone for one-hour breaks in order to get warm.

While out on the ship's bow one night, Elwell's most memorable sight in that region was the display of the northern lights. He described them as beautiful, sparkling, and of every color. There was one thing he was not fond of and that was the six months of darkness experienced in the northern Atlantic. Utterly depressing!

He recalls the one time he became quite homesick. It was when he heard over the ship's loudspeaker the familiar song, "Easter Parade." That caused him to recollect the good times he'd had while growing up in Alabama.

The men on the ship all raved about the food – the best in the Navy. They especially loved the pies produced by a baker nicknamed 'Dough Head.'

A black cat named 'Eight Ball' was the ship's mascot giving the crew many hours of pleasure. She had the run of the ship, wearing her own personalized dog tag hanging from a collar around her neck. Regrettably on one trip into

I Was There

Greenland, Eight Ball came up missing. The ship's captain sent out a crew to search for her. She was never found. Some believed that the crew on another ship that was tied up nearby was now enjoying her company.

On a voyage into the North Atlantic from Narsarssuak, Greenland to St John's, Newfoundland, the Laramie and six other ships escorted by the United States Coast Guard Cutter (USCGC) Escanaba hit weather considered bad even for the North Atlantic. They had to skirt the ice fields by proceeding northwest along the coastline for a while. The Laramie was loaded with three-hundred sixty-one gallons of aviation gasoline, fifty-five thousand barrels of oil and general cargo.

When the convoy reached the eastern end of Belle Isle Strait, the Laramie was positioned to the right of the Escanaba. A seaman aboard the Escanaba heard what he thought was the sound of gear tracking a torpedo. A moment later a terrific explosion ripped through the cutter.

It was five a.m. and the explosion and sinking happened within three minutes, so rapidly that the captain never had time to signal its plight. Two men were picked up from the freezing water and the rest of the crew died in the explosion or from hypothermia.

Those crew members awake and on duty on the Laramie watched in shock as this horrific explosion took place. At that moment, Elwell was on gun watch on the port side using binoculars to observe the day break and also to keep an eye out for trails of water from enemy submarine periscopes. He stood mesmerized by what happened right in front of his eyes.

I Was There

Then within minutes, the Laramie was T-boned on the port side forward by a torpedo. It just missed the engine room and sleeping quarters. She immediately listed to the port side and went down by the bow some thirty-seven feet. The blast demolished the forward crew's quarters, killing several men and opened a hole forty-one feet long and thirty-four feet high.

Lives lost - buried at sea

I Was There

The forward had extensive flooding and the port gasoline tank sprayed the ship with volatile liquid and explosive fumes. Despite imminent danger of explosion and flooding, the commander took action to save the Laramie, even though gasoline ran ankle-deep over the forward gun platforms.

Crippled, the ship made it to Sydney, Nova Scotia escorted by the USCGC Mohawk before she headed to Boston a few days later for repairs.

When asked what duties the crew performed while in dry dock, with a grin Elwell said, "Chip and paint everything in sight to include painting the sides of the ship. If it don't speak or move, it got painted."

Ships Serviceman Second Class Lee Elwell was discharged in November 1946 and headed back to Alabama and Catherine. There he secured a job with U.S. Steel as a crane operator. Later, he would do a six-year stint with the Birmingham Police Department. The low pay forced him to have a side job and consequently saw little of his family.

By this time Lee and Catherine had two boys, Lee E. Elwell, III and Robin. When Robin was twelve years old, he was killed in a car accident when a drunk driver going over seventy miles-an-hour broadsided the family's car where Robin was sitting. The car was totaled even though it was a heavy built Oldsmobile. The whole family was rushed to the hospital, but Robin did not survive.

In 1964, the family bought a piece of property in Panama City Beach where they built a home, and son Lee built his home on the adjoining property.

Catherine passed away in 2005, and in 2009 Lee had to move to Sims Veterans' Home for health reasons.

I Was There

Lee Elwell is the president of the Residents' Council at Sims, an intermediary position between the residents and the staff of the Veterans' Home.

His happy demeanor along with his broad smile is a big asset to the daily routine that takes place at the Veterans' Home.

I Was There

Lt. Col. Walter T. Wilson
was there at the
Normandy Invasion

Walter Wilson was there when the U.S. military stormed the beaches at Normandy in June, 1944. Now ninety-six years old, he recalls the day in 1940 when he received his draft notice to report to the Army. Born in 1915 in Augusta, Georgia, Walter was working as a hotel manager at the Peabody Hotel in Memphis, Tennessee, when he got his call to serve his country. His basic training took place at Ft. Bragg, North Carolina. He then attended Officer Candidate School (OCS) and graduated as a Second Lieutenant and was assigned to the 2nd Armored Division at Ft. Bragg, North Carolina.

I Was There

The 2nd Armored Division was sent on an overseas mission to the invasion of Morocco in 1942. Next they were sent to the invasion of Sicily in 1943. From there they moved to England. The Division was stationed at Tidworth, Wiltshire County, England, a few kilometers from the legendary monument, Stonehenge. Tidworth was also the base for England's 1st Mechanical Brigade. Now a captain, Wilson was sent there with his battalion to outfit the tanks in preparation for the Normandy invasion of German-held France.

The Invasion of Normandy was made up of Allied Forces consisting of the United States, United Kingdom, Canada, Free French Forces, Free Polish Forces, Australia, Free Belgian Forces, New Zealand, Netherlands, Norway, Free Czechoslovak Forces and Greece. Most of these countries would also provide air and naval support.

For months leading up to the invasion, the allied forces conducted a deceptive operation codenamed Operation Fortitude, a mission aimed at misleading the date and place of the invasion that the German's were expecting. The Allies assigned codenames to the various operations involved in the invasion. *Overlord* was the name assigned to the establishment of a large-scale placement on the northern position of the European continent. Allied forces rehearsed their roles for D-Day months before the invasion.

The invasion actually began the previous day with overnight parachute and glider landings along with massive air attacks and naval bombardments. Then early on the morning of June 6^{th,} amphibious landings began on five beaches codenamed *Juno, Gold, Omaha, Utah* and *Sword.*

I Was There

When the call came in England for the 2nd Armored Division to advance forward with *Operation Overlord*, Wilson, now a major, rallied his battalion of young and scared, but well trained men to proceed to Landing Ship, Tanks (LSTs) that would take them cross the English Channel to Normandy. Their assignment was to land on Omaha Beach.

As the LST crossed the Channel, there were four men in each tank: the tank commander, driver, assistant driver, and the gunner. They hunkered down, awaiting and anticipating the battle that lay ahead of them.

At daybreak, as they neared the landing sight, Major Wilson scanned the waters in front of the LST and could not believe the scene before him. He was awed by the huge flotilla of five thousand ships already poised and ready for war. Battleships that were positioned the farthest from shore were already pounding the hillside with gunfire at German gun placements, preparing the way for Allied troops to storm the beach. When asked if he was scared, Walter Wilson's quick reply was, "We didn't have time to think about anything else but the objective: to invade."

Omaha Beach is six miles wide and the largest of the five beaches that would be invaded. The entire beach was overlooked by cliffs. That made attacking the area very difficult for the Allies, as German gun emplacements had been well positioned all long those cliffs. The enemy, too, had begun their anti-invasion maneuvers the night before D-Day, and was on high alert when it started.

The Germans were largely deployed in strongpoints along the coast in concrete bunkers. They had also built a steel barrier in the water adjacent to the shoreline where it

I Was There

could not be seen. The LSTs would have to clear those barriers in order to move forward close to ashore. Many did not make it across and had to unload men and tanks into the water.

As the LST carrying Wilson and his men moved forward, dead bodies of Allied troops could be seen floating in the water. Those men had been direct targets for German machine guns and artillery from the cliffs above.

Many more men lay on the beach either dead or wounded while others hobbled toward safety after being hit. Valiantly, wounded men tried to go back into the water to help their injured comrade to shore but would invariably be hit again by enemy fire. It was a horrific scene witnessed by those still coming ashore. A real bloodbath ensued. Even so, it was the first breakthrough for the Allied forces.

When the LST hit the shoreline of Omaha Beach they opened the huge front doors, and Walter Wilson's big Sherman tank, followed by the others, moved out and onto the shore. He did his best to fulfill his assignment to keep radio contact with the other tanks to inform them of further instructions. As tank commander, his job included watching through the open hatch at the top of the tank to warn the driver of impending danger, a difficult task to be sure. The battle at Omaha Beach raged on with approximately one-hundred men from Wilson's battalion killed during the eleven days they battled the Germans.

After that long battle and the beach secured, Wilson's next assignment was to lead his battalion toward the German-fortified French city of Saint Lo. His orders were to advance at six a.m. *only* after seven-hundred planes had dropped bombs onto the area. The instructions to the aircraft above was to drop only light bombs so as not to make big craters upon impact, which would have impeded the fast movement forward by the tanks. When the last bomb was dropped, Wilson's battalion moved in for the attack.

Sherman Tank

The tanks had moved from Omaha Beach crawling over hills that were fairly clear of trees and underbrush until they reached the outskirts of Saint Lo. Using their cannons and machine guns, the battalion went to work to liberate the city. It took two full weeks of continuous fighting to do so. Taking one city block at a time, men were sent into homes checking room-by-room for Germans or any sign of life. The city was already in ruins, and dead bodies were strewn everywhere.

When the last house was found to be void of Germans, Major Wilson's battalion moved on. They plowed through France, moving from town-to-town and skirmish-to-skirmish capturing German soldiers. The battle at Saint Lo remains in Walter Wilson's mind as the most memorable but also extremely heart-rending for all the loss of men that occurred.

During the mission, the men had little time for anything but eating the C-rations stored in the tight space within a tank's inner core. A change of clothing was as rare as a hot meal or a hot shower. On one maneuver in France, Wilson and his men were knocked about when their tank hit a mine. The men received cuts and bruises, and the damage to the tank was limited to the tracks being torn from it.

After the invasion of Saint Lo, the 2nd Armored Division's commanding officer, Lieutenant General Edward H. Brooks, was transferred to the south of France as III Corps Commander. Major Wilson was transferred with him as his aide. It was there that Major Wilson advanced to Lieutenant Colonel. He remained as an aide until the end of the war.

In 1947 he was discharged and put into the honorary status of the Army Reserves, to be called back to duty in case of an emergency. During Walter's Army career he earned the Bronze Star with cluster, four battle ribbons and the Silver Star.

After being released from the Army, Walter went back to work at the Peabody Hotel in Memphis, Tennessee where he had worked prior to being drafted. Then, using the government sponsored G.I. Bill, Walter then obtained a degree in mathematics from the University of North Carolina. He had planned to use his education toward a career in the hotel business. Instead of those plans, Walter chose to work at Contract Bridge, traveling around the United States promoting the game of bridge. His office was in Memphis where he managed a monthly bridge magazine

I Was There

and also planned nation-wide contests and kept the scores for all the participants.

Later, Walter moved to Panama City where he was asked to share his war experiences with local high school students. The interest in his story and the response from the teenagers was gratifying to Walter.

Also satisfying to him is when he is able to enjoy the company of and conversations with visitors as well as other veterans who share the Sims Veterans' Home with him. Walter Wilson still enjoys a good cigar and a stimulating game of bridge.

◀▶

I Was There

CPO Willie N. Taylor
was there to teach personnel
to assemble and replace temporary
steel landing strips for the war zones

Ninety-eight year old Willie Taylor recalls when he was in the Seabees and relates those days to whoever will listen. Born in 1913 at Marianna, Florida, he finished elementary school but there was no high school at that time, so his education came to a halt. To occupy his time, he went to work at a local shipyard repairing boats.

Prior to the war being declared with Japan, an opportunity presented itself for him to work for the DuPont Company at the Panama Canal. It was there they he learned to attach eighteen-inch steel armor plates for bomb-proofing the locks and heavy machinery. Later, when the company downsized, he asked to be transferred back to the states and was given an assignment at Hanford, Washington, at the DuPont Atomic Plant for the *Manhattan Project.*

The United States government had become concerned about the scientists in Nazi Germany who were developing a nuclear weapons program. Therefore, in 1942, the Army Corps of Engineers placed the newly formed *Manhattan Project* under the command of General Leslie R. Groves. He was charged with the construction of industrial-size plants for manufacturing plutonium and uranium. The general chose the DuPont Company to be the prime contractor for the construction of the plutonium production complex.

General Groves had dispatched his assistant Colonel Franklin T. Matthias and DuPont engineers to scout potential sites. Matthias reported that Hanford, Washington was ideal in virtually all aspects and it was near the Columbia River and also the Pacific Ocean. A month later that site was established as the Hanford Engineer Works, codenamed "Site W." The land was quickly acquired under the eminent domain authority, and some fifteen hundred residents of Hanford and nearby settlements of Indian tribes were relocated.

The *Manhattan Project* developed the atomic bomb that was dropped on Hiroshima on August 6, 1945. The bomb called "Little Boy," was made primarily of plutonium-239, a synthetic element created at Hanford, Washington.

When Taylor worked in Panama, he did not have to register for the draft. But as soon as he moved to the State of Washington to work at the Hanford atomic plant the U.

I Was There

S. directive became a must for him. He had to drive to Spokane, Washington, a round trip of three-hundred-forty miles to register for the draft. The roads were in poor condition, and the temperature outside a real scorcher. Even that far back, he had an air conditioned car. Of course, it wasn't at the flick of a switch like that of today where cool air blows at the temperature of your pleasure. His makeshift apparatus was a can filled with ice that he held out the window and let the wind blow through it. He still chuckles today telling that story.

He would drive to Spokane draft board office every six months to find out if his 'number was up.' Finally he decided that Uncle Sam would soon draft him for the Army, so he chose to volunteer. He was also quite aware that he had a choice of being drafted at a salary of sixty-dollars per month or volunteering at a monthly pay of one hundred twenty-four dollars and fifty cents. You probably already guessed which one this young man would take.

He drove to Spokane and was at the recruiting office even before the door opened. His first words to the recruiter were, "I'm a getting' tired of working nights. What've you got to offer me in the service?" After looking at Willie's resume of previous jobs, the recruiter's reply was, "If you can wait until next month I can give you a Lieutenant Junior Grade (Lt. JG) assignment."

Willie had no idea what that meant, but knew that if he waited a month, he might get drafted. So he asked, "What else have you got?"

I Was There

Seabees

Willie joined the Seabees and his first assignment was at Providence, Rhode Island where his unit practiced assembling and laying down steel mats that measured twelve feet long by six feet wide. They were used as temporary runways for the landing sites in all types of terrain in the Pacific Theater of Operations.

At the end of each steel mat was a curved lip that turned down on one end and the adjoining mat curved up, thereby enabling them to join together. The mats were extremely heavy and a great deal of human strength was needed to connect two of them together. Willie got scratched by one of the mats during one of those connections and gangrene soon set in and landed him in the hospital for two weeks.

According to a report by Calamet Industries, manufacturer of the steel mat, the United States manufactured during the war a quantity of landing mats capable of building a roadway around the world's equator – enough steel to build six-hundred and fifty ten-thousand ton cargo ships.

Willie rose to the rank of Chief Petty Officer (CPO) in Providence and was placed in charge of teaching a two-week course on how to assemble those mats to troops who would be shipping out to the war zone. This was necessary training, as if a crippled plane came in for a crash landing, it could easily take out a quarter of a mile of the temporary

I Was There

runway. Those damaged sections of mats would then need to be replaced - immediately.

When CPO Taylor was discharged at the end of the war, he returned to Hanford, Washington, to work for DuPont for the next two years. That company later was taken over by General Electric.

He quit General Electric after a period of time and worked for companies just outside of Portland, Oregon. He had to join the Mill Wright Union, as Oregon is quite a union state. He is still a lifetime member of that union. He installed turbines in a hydro-power plant on the Columbia River, which separates Washington, Oregon and Idaho. That particular company produced the machinery and installed those units. Taylor's position was to oversee the installation. The units could not be plus or minus two one-hundreds of an inch off, a very exacting and delicate job. He had to answer for anything that was not up to specification.

His civilian career took him from positions of installing computerized machinery at a saw mill to the Colorado Fuel and Iron Company in Portland, Oregon. He retired in 1988 at age seventy-five from Alcoa Aluminum where he helped install machinery for making beer cans.

In the positions that Taylor held in each company, he always excelled, generally as a supervisor over highly skilled projects and with only an eighth-grade education.

Willie Taylor is the father of two daughters from his first wife, Dellia. One lives in Atlanta, Georgia and the other in Portland, Oregon. He is blessed to hear from them at least twice a day.

I Was There

When Taylor turned ninety he met Velma, also ninety, and married her in Franklin, North Carolina. They spent winters in Panama City, Florida and summers in Georgia until his health caused him to move to the Sims Veterans' Home.

At ninety-seven Willie Taylor is a spry gentleman who keeps himself busy with all kinds of projects during the day and loves to play board games in the activity room with a group of men. His wife Velma still lives in their winter home in Panama City. Taylor would rather be at home with her, but his health precludes that. So he made up his mind to enjoy his new surroundings.

I Was There

T/Sgt. Edward A. Reinholtz
was there as a
B-17 Right Waist Gunner
during bombing raids over Germany

Edward Reinholtz was born in 1921 at Middletown, Connecticut, located on the western bank of the Connecticut River. At age eighteen, Edward enlisted in the Army Air Corps and took his basic training at Ft. Meyers, Florida. He left behind his beloved sweetheart, but also left behind the thing which he loved to do – ride horses. He had been an instructor for the Connecticut Horse Show Association and the LB Riding Club.

Because of this love of horses, he requested to be a part of the Army's Calvary Division, but there were no openings at that time. He was then sent to Langley Field, Virginia for training at a gunnery school to become an

51

expert with the guns and also repairman. It was there that the men were selected for individual crews and trained for the B-24 (later for the B-17) and where he was given the job of armorer nose gunner. On January 7, 1942, Reinholtz went home on leave and married Marian Johnson, his sweetheart since grade school. Marian, of course, stayed behind when he returned to his squadron.

Reinholtz's crew was sent on a Boeing B-17 Flying Fortress to an American base in South American to await further orders to proceed to Europe. As is per usual in military life, they had to *hurry up* to get there and then *wait* for further instructions. Soon orders were received to head for Foggia, Italy. It was the jumping off place for the planes to hasten for action over Africa and Europe. He was assigned to the 15th Air Force, 96th Bomb Group – Jimmy Doolittle's squadron during World War I.

The B-17s were used by the United States Army Air Force primarily for bombing campaigns against German industrial and military targets. The intent and effect was to put them out of business.

B-17s had become the most popular plane in World War II. The four engine heavy bomber planes were generally named by the ground crews that had to repair them. This was due to the fact that when a plane came in from a mission all shot up by the Germans; the repairmen had to spend a great deal of time restoring it back into service. Besides engine repair many hours were spent in plugging up bullet holes of all sizes. It was nothing for a plane to return to base camp with hundreds of bullet holes in its body.

Since the ground crew chief and his men spend so many hours repairing an individual plane they were the ones that usually named the B-17s. Names like *Memphis Belle*, *Eight Ball* and *Rosie's Riveters* were painted in huge letters on the side of the plane. Sgt. Reinholtz flew in the *Immortal Crew* – so named because everyone survived. (Side note: Film actor, Clark Gable flew five missions as waist gunner in the *Eight Ball* in 1943. Earlier that year, as a first lieutenant, he spent five weeks at Tyndall AFB, Florida in gunner school.)

The B-17s were equipped with thirteen machine gun mounts. The guns used .50-caliber shells and the gunner could only shoot five rounds at a time with a pause in between. A carriage was in place to prevent more rounds from being fired at one time as the gun itself would become so hot it would melt.

Ten-man crews flew the B-17; pilot, co-pilot, navigator, bombardier, flight engineer/top turret gunner, five other gunner positions: nose, tail, left and right waist, and ball turret. Reinholtz's position was that of the right waist gunner's station – on the right side of the plane where he stood behind a Plexiglas window with the gun placement at waist high. His assignment was to watch for enemy planes approaching on the right side of the plane.

I Was There

Certain squadrons were sent on shuttle runs, and the 96th Squadron was one of them. The plane would leave the base near Foggia fueled up and loaded with bombs. They dropped their bomb load on the designated sight in Germany, fly on to Romania, where Russian ground crews refueled and reloaded bombs onto the plane. Reinholtz stated that the American B-17 crews were quite skeptical of the Russian Ground crews, not able to trust them, always wondering if they were friend or foe.

The plane would then leave Romania, drop a load of bombs over Germany and fly on to England where they would again refuel and reload bombs. They took off from England and bombed Germany as the plane made its way back to base camp in Italy.

Along with each mission, came the fear of 'no return'. Fighter escorts flew with the formation of B-17s to and from the target. Sgt. Reinholtz commented that the amount of flak received from the ground and German fighter planes during the flight across Germany was unreal, and especially when one of the planes from the squadron got a direct hit and began to spiral downward. Only when they sighted parachutes did the crew breathe a sigh of relief. His brother-in-law's B-17 was shot down and he was captured and spent quite some time in a contemptible German prisoner of war camp.

On one mission out of Foggia, Italy, Reinholtz's crew flew a mission into Yugoslavia and on to Romania, where the target was the oil storage tanks where the Germans got their fuel. While in retreat from that area they were surprised by unexpected anti-aircraft fire from placements on trains that followed the squadron. Nine bombers were shot down, with ninety men killed.

On one mission where his crew had to shuttle into the Ukraine, they landed, refueled and then took off again for their main target in Romania. While heading home the plane ran out of fuel. The pilot brought the plane and the frightened crew in to land on an emergency runway on one of the islands in the Mediterranean. The end of the airstrip sloped into the water, and that is the spot where the pilot put the plane down. When the wheels touch down, the tail gunner's position was now dragging in the water. However impossible it looked, the pilot brought it in safely.

The bombs used on the B-17 were five-hundred pound armor piercing bombs. Sgt. Reinholtz was also trained to fill in as bombardier. On one particular flight from Romania, he had to check out the bomb bay to make sure all the bombs had cleared the plane. One was still hanging, almost by a thread. The pilot had to find a target that wasn't a city, so it could be dropped.

Sgt. Reinholtz declares that he had the best crew in the Air Force, with Squadron Commander George Chadwick as pilot and co-pilot George Morris on the *Immortal Crew*.

Foggia wasn't a bad place to be stationed, Sgt. Reinholtz reported. The men lived in tents but living among the Italian people was okay as they were good people. Men on leave would go into town to a few of the bars where the Italians catered to the servicemen.

The men could also take a boat trip to the Isle of Capri. The Blue Grotto was a favorite stop when visiting on the Isle. It is one of several sea caves, worldwide, that is flooded with a brilliant blue and emerald light. That light comes from a hole that is barely large enough to allow a tiny rowboat to get through.

To enter that low opening to the grotto, one transfers from the motorized boat that brought him or her from the port into a small wooden rowboat manned by an oarsman. Because there is no headroom, visitors must lay on their backs in the bottom of the rowboats as they clear the entranceway. Once inside, the grotto is quite roomy and one is able to sit upright.

Another tourist attraction on the island is at the top of Capo, where stands the ruins of twelve villas once occupied by Emperor Tiberius Caesar. The view from atop that mountain of the Gulf of Naples is awesome.

On a five-day pass, Sgt. Reinholtz studied the architecture of Rome. While there, he had the privilege to meet and shake hands with Pope Pius XII. The pope spoke only one sentence to him but the words stayed with him throughout his time in the service: "You're going to make it all right."

He visited the Sistine Chapel and was awed by the paintings on the ceilings and walls, especially Michelangelo's *Last Judgment* where the renowned painter had to lay on his back to paint. Another favorite was the image of the Hand of God giving life to Adam.

T/Sgt. Reinholtz completed fifty missions while at Foggia, and was eligible for discharge in 1945. He left the 15th Air Force and headed back to Middleton, Connecticut.

His first job was as a mechanic on oil burners in homes, and following that he became Chief Engineer over seven maintenance men at a psychiatric hospital in Portland, Connecticut. Later he worked as heating engineer at Bacon

I Was There

Brothers Plumbing and Heating. His wife, Marian, was the secretary to the boss, and Edward found all kinds of reasons for going to her office. Even after all those years since grade school he was still smitten with this lovely lady.

Edward spends his time at the Veterans' Home visiting with other residents and enjoying regular visits from his son, who lives in Port St. Joe, Florida.

◄►

I Was There

I Was There

On the Home Front

1941-1945

The men and women in uniform who served during World War II made great sacrifices. Because of that, few back home complained of the daily sacrifices they had to make. The men, whose stories are in this book, along with the hundreds of thousands of others, left behind mothers, fathers, sisters, brothers, relatives, friends and neighbors who put up a united front in their efforts to help with the war effort.

Civilian men walked the streets of neighborhoods as "Civil Defense air raid wardens." Their duty was to enforce the ruling that all windows be blacked out to prevent any light from penetrating the darkness. Armed only with a flashlight and a whistle, they checked every home and ever window as residents sometimes forgot about a small window in the basement or other area of the house that was not covered. They also saw to it that street lights, store signs and emergency lights were turned off.

A person couldn't just walk into a store and buy food items they needed or wanted, nor could they fill up their car with gasoline whenever they liked. Those things were rationed because of the shortage of supply. The government felt that rationing was the only way to make sure everyone got their fair share. A member of each family was asked to register for coupons for each person in the family. Each person was allowed a certain amount of points weekly with expiration dates to consider.

Red Stamp coupons covered all meats, butter, fat and oils. Blue Stamps were used for canned, bottled, frozen fruits and vegetables, plus juices, dry beans, baby food and ketchup. Each stamp was worth so many points.

Points on #2 Can of Vegetables
Peas (1 lb. 4 oz.)   16 points

Points on Fruits
Peaches (1 lb. 14 oz.)   21 points

One book of stamps to each
family member

The April 20, 1942 issue of *Life Magazine* printed the following article:

Uncle Sam last week assumed the role of fashion designer. Sweeping restrictions aim to save fifteen percent of the yardage now used on

I Was There

women's and girls' apparel through such measures as restricting hems and belts to two inches, eliminating cuffs on sleeves. Exempt categories include bridal gowns, maternity dresses and vestments for religious orders.

Much to the chagrin of women was the shortage of nylon for their stockings, as nylon was being used for military parachutes. Ingenuity arose to the occasion when department stores provided mending for those inevitable runs in nylons.

Citizens were asked to contribute scrap rubber to be recycled; old tires, old rubber raincoats, garden hoses, rubber shoes and bathing caps.

The U.S. War Production Board (1942) sent out the following emergency statement:

In spite of the recent rubber drive, there is a continuing need for large quantities of scrap rubber. We are collecting every possible pound from the factories, arsenals and ships; we are speeding up the flow of material from automobile graveyards; we are tearing up abandoned railroad tracks and bridges, but unless we dig out an additional six million tons of steel and great quantities of rubber, copper, brass, zinc and tin, our boys may not get all the fighting weapons they need in time . . . Even one old shovel will help make four hand grenades.

I Was There

Half the U.S. automobiles were issued an 'A' sticker which allowed *four gallons* of fuel *per week*. The 'B' sticker was for driving deemed essential to the war effort such as industrial workers. The maximum speed was set at thirty-five miles-per-hour.

Citizens were encouraged to purchase war bonds and stamps to supplement monies for the war effort. War bond drives were prevalent in cities around the U.S., with popular movie stars on hand urging citizens to purchase the bonds. In the schools, children purchased stamps to fill stamp books toward a bond.

New on the home front was the advent of women in the work place. At first, industry leaders frowned upon the contribution women *could* make in replacing men who went to war. But when their blinded eyes saw their male workers leave in droves after being called up by their local draft board, those skeptics had to concede to hiring women.

Women rolled up their sleeves and went to work driving taxis and garbage trucks, and handling jobs in the lumber industry as cooks and lumberjacks. Others trained to become welders and riveters in the production of military planes, tanks and trucks.

Women welders

Meat markets hired women to cut-up carcasses of beef while farms employed women to milk cows, slop the hogs and bale hay.

Millions of women joined the Red Cross as nurses' aides and drove ambulances. Others worked in USO canteens providing food and entertainment to troops here in the States. _____

News report of the attack on Pearl Harbor must have inflicted great torment upon families of servicemen stationed there. The 'not knowing' was so difficult to handle. *Is my son/husband alive or dead?* Picture yourself reading in the newspaper the day after the attack the number of ship casualties of those docked at Pearl Harbor:

Arizona - sunk

California – sunk

Casin – heavily damaged

Curtis – damaged

I Was There

Downs – heavily damaged
Helm - damaged
Honolulu - damaged
Maryland - damaged
Nevada – heavily damaged
Oglala - sunk
Oklahoma – capsized
Pennsylvania – slightly damaged
Raleigh – heavily damaged
Shaw – severely damaged
Sotoyono (harbor tug) - sunk
Tennessee - damaged
Utah - sunk
Vestal – heavily damaged
West Virginia – sunk
Three hundred fifty aircraft damaged

Hickam Field and other military sites on Oahu were severely damaged.

Sheer torture set in for the loved ones as they waited for a letter or phone call to say their son, husband, uncle or nephew was okay. They might not hear any news for days or even weeks. *Did my loved one survive the attack?* That same desperate cry of the heart to know must have occurred over and over again as attacks were made upon Guadalcanal, Midway and the other islands in the Pacific and also during the invasion at Normandy in the Atlantic. When the mail did arrive it was censored with huge black lines marked through sentences for security purposes. The reader could only surmise what had been said under the obliteration, which brought fear and anguish.

I Was There

Seeing uniformed men approach the front door of a home was another fear held in the bosom of loved ones. It was an obvious sign of death. That scene played over and over in the mind of an individual as he/she waited daily for news of their loved one.

Those on the *Home Front* sacrificed much, but nothing like those in the trenches, in tanks, fighter jets, bombers, naval vessels and submarines. But thankfully, in a united effort the men and women and even the children of the United States worked together to help support our troops.

The unity that transpired in the efforts to back the men and women in uniform was overwhelming throughout the United States. One we never experienced before or since. Citizens gladly gave military hitch hikers a ride – even if it took the drivers out of their way. Service personnel stationed at bases in the U.S. were invited to share dinner with a family -- even as sparse as it might be. A man in uniform standing around on a street corner was invited to attend some function being held in town – a dance or a free baseball game. Those men were grateful for the love and support an unknown individual provided at that lonely moment.

Those on the home front are among the unsung heroes of World War II. They are to be saluted for their many efforts.

◀▶

I Was There

War had ended in the Europe, but it took several days before the Germans would surrender on all fronts. It all began with the execution of Benito Mussolini that took place on April 27, 1945, after he tried to flee from Italy to Switzerland. Then Adolph Hitler committed suicide on April 30th. In his will he appointed Admiral Karl Dönitz as the new President of Germany and Joseph Goebbels as the Chancellor of Germany. Goebbels committed suicide on May 1, 1945. That same day the German forces in Italy surrendered, German troops in Berlin surrendered on the 2nd, which was followed on May 4th by the surrender in North West Germany, Denmark and the Netherlands. For the next succeeding days the Germans armed forces in all areas finally surrendered.

In the United States, the news of the surrender was broadcast on May 8th, with that day declared as V-E Day – Victory in Europe. However, the country was still at war in the Pacific.

◄►

Japan Surrenders

The mushroom cloud made by the Atomic bomb

The year after the war had begun in the Pacific, the U.S. army was looking for a remote area for a top-secret project.

They found what they were looking for thirty-five miles northwest of Santa Fe, New Mexico in the area of Los Alamos. It had been chosen as the 'Manhattan Projects' central laboratory because of its isolated location.

A town was built with prefabricated housing, trailers and Quonset huts ready for the scientists and their families to move into. The population of that small city grew to five thousand in a short period of time. Barbed wire circled the fifty-four thousand acre site and was heavily guarded.

Laboratories were set up to build the world's first reactor that used uranium. A test site known as 'Trinity' was built on a stretch of the Alamogordo Bombing Range to foretell the bombs future. For the next three years, scientists worked to perfect an atomic bomb.

Upon the death of President Franklin D. Roosevelt on April 12, 1945, Vice President Harry Truman had to step into his predecessor's shoes in the midst of two wars. Only on the day Truman assumed presidency was he told of the secret weapon with extraordinary power being developed. Two weeks later he was faced with the awesome decision as to what to do with that power.

In the meantime, the military waited for further instructions from the President, to proceed with plans to drop "Little Boy" on Japan. On the island of Tinian in the western Pacific, Colonel Tibbets was given the task of master-minding the bombing campaign. He carefully handpicked his crew. They would have no knowledge until the last moment that their flight was carrying an atomic bomb nicknamed "Little Boy".

Earlier, The U.S.S. Indianapolis had been given the task for sailing across the Pacific with "Little Boy" and "Fat Man" as cargo. They were to deliver them to Tinian Island for loading onto two B-29s. That task called for extremely careful handling of the two bombs.

In the devastated city of Berlin, President Truman was attending the Potsdam Conference where the Big Three – the United States, Britain and the Russia - were meeting to discuss how to best deal with war-torn Europe. Truman could only hope to also discuss the subject of ending the war in the Pacific.

But he received no backing from the Soviets regarding the Pacific war. Therefore, Truman knew he must plunge ahead with "Little Boy".

I Was There

On August 6, 1945, Colonel Tibbets was given the signal to go forward with the plan to drop "Little Boy" on Hiroshima, Japan. It weighed over four and a half tons and took great skill in loading it aboard the plane. The B-29 had the words "Enola Gay" painted on its nose – in honor of Colonel Tibbets' grandmother.

The bomb was meticulously dropped that day and yet missed the target by eight hundred feet. The devastation on the ground that followed was almost incomprehensible. Having completed the mission, the bomb bay doors were closed on the Enola Gay and Colonel Tibbets breathed a huge sigh of relief. He then turned the plane around and headed back to Tinian Island.

Only after the bomb was released on Hiroshima was Tibbets' entire unit back on the island told of the secret mission. When the Enola Gay taxied down the runway and pulled onto the tarmac Tibbets and his crew saw the huge crowded that had gathered to welcome them home.

Three days later on August 9, 1945, Major Charles Sweeney piloted a B-29 named "Bock's Car" to Nagasaki, Japan carrying "Fat Boy" a large shaped plutonium bomb in its bomb bay. That day the target was missed by over a mile, but still produced the projected outcome – Japan's surrender.

The war and continual bloodshed in the Pacific was finally over.

I Was There

WAR in EUROPE

World War II Timeline

September 1939: German Invasion of Poland

August 1940: Battle of Britain – RAF vs. Luftwaffe

February 1941: German Afrika Korps arrives in N. Africa

June 1941: Third Reich Invades the USSR

December 1941: Japanese attack Pearl Harbor

June 1942: Battle of Midway in the Pacific

November 1942: Americans open 2nd Front in N. Africa

November 1942: Battle of Stalingrad

July 1943: Anglo-American Landings in Sicily

March 1944: Japanese attack British India

June 1944: D-Day – Allied Invasion of Normandy

October 1944: American Liberation of the Philippines

December 1944: Battle of the Bulge in the Ardennes

February 1945: American Landings on Iwo Jima

April 1945: U.S. Invasion of Okinawa

April 1945: Battle of Berlin – End of the Third Reich

August 1945: Japan Surrenders

I Was There

Korean Conflict

Stories

**Korean Memorial in
Washington D.C.**

The Korean Conflict

Tension between the Soviet Union and the United States heightened at the end of World War II. The U.S. feared that the Soviet Union intended to propagate communism to other nations.

In 1950, the Korean Peninsula was divided between a Soviet-backed government in the north and an American-backed government in the south. That division came about at the end of World War II. The United States feared that the Soviet Union would take over the entire peninsula, so it quickly moved its own troops into southern Korea.

The United States and the Soviet Union agreed to divide Korea temporarily along the 38th parallel, a latitudinal line that intersected the country. In 1946, a communist government was formed in the north called the Democratic People's Republic headed by Kim Il Sung. Soon after, the Republic of Korea (ROK) was established in the south.

War broke out along the 38th parallel on June 25, 1950. North Korean troops headed south to Seoul on that day. The United Nations Security Council adopted a resolution condemning the invasion. President Harry Truman committed American military to a combined United Nations military effort of fifteen other nations. The Truman administration was determined not to lose another country to communism.

◄►

PFC Michael R. Mancos
was there in Korea at
Pork Chop Hill and Old Baldy

101st Airborne

Michael Mancos was born in 1932 in Trebisov, Czechoslovakia, in the eastern part of what is now Slovakia. He emigrated to Ecorse, Michigan with his parents at the age of three.

Mancos was drafted into the Army in 1952, willing to go to war for the country that had now become his country. He took basic training at Breckenridge, Kentucky with the 101st Air Borne. His MOS (Military Operation Specialty) was – rifleman.

It just so happened, that several men and Michael Mancos were not American citizens at the time of enlistment. At their *swearing-in* for military service, they first had to *swear-in* to become a citizen of the United States. A sergeant spoke to those men who were lined up, saying, "Seven men at a time step to the other side of the chalk line." The men all looked around at each other, and then seven men stepped forward and across that chalk line. "Now, raise your right hand and repeat after me. I ... " The emigrant recruits spoke their name and continued to repeat the oath, swearing to the allegiance to the United States of America. "Now step back across the chalk line. You are now citizens of the United States of America." Turning to the crowd he then said, "Next seven step across to the other side of the chalk line." Mancos couldn't help but smile as he crossed back over that line on the floor. He was now a full-fledged American.

———

Before leaving for Korea, he was sent to Camp Drake on Japan's Etajima Island for eight weeks training as a field lineman. He learned the basics in laying and repairing wire used to connect radios and telephones while in the field. Since the training was for his deployment to Korea, he trained in caves, on hills and mountains which depicted the terrain in that country. He had to climb telephone poles and learn how to run new communication lines should the Chinese blow them up and they had to be replaced.

While at Camp Drake, Mancos visited Hiroshima where he saw the devastation that still prevailed in that city - the result of the atomic bomb dropped there by the United States. In the seven years since that bombing, nothing had been reconstructed -- everything had been left as it happened on August 6, 1945. That act of war forced the Japanese to surrender.

After eight weeks of training at Camp Drake, his unit was put aboard a ship heading to Pusan, Korea at the very southern tip of what is now South Korea. They crossed the Sea of Japan in the darkness of night, so as not to be seen.

The boatload of troops arrived in the rain soaked mud hole of Pusan on March 1953. With duffle bag in hand they boarded a train that was painted black and there were no panes in the windows – they had been shot out. Half-inch steel had been attached to the outside of each car under the window frames. Those measures were taken because of the bullets fired by the Chinese at the trains. The men were immediately ordered to lie on the floor and absolutely no cigarettes were to be smoked. Mancos recalled one fella saying "Don't mean me" and lit up. A sergeant hit him in the head with the butt of a rifle. The cigarette was immediately extinguished.

The army could only hope to get the train load of men to the front lines of the war without casualties. Hundreds of bullet holes were already visible in the body of the train and also in the ceiling and the walls of the inside. The men laid there, cold and wet, as the rain came through the pane less windows. The men kept their heads as low as possible. Their bodies were rigid with fear as the bullets came zinging through those open windows.

Mancos stated that, as a young man, what was happening all around them didn't seem real - more like watching a war movie. He and the others were not ready to experience all of this. They stayed in that position on the floor during the entire trip to the north, approximately six hours.

After his unit left the train, the men marched in freezing rain for over a mile to the 38th parallel. There they were joined with the 7th Army Infantry Division which had lost so many men. They were freezing cold even though they were wearing winter gear.

The first full day after the unit arrived, Chinese loud speakers blasted out the words: "Welcome American soldiers. Hope you have a good vacation. Soon you will die." Then they began to read the names of everyone who had just arrived the day before.

The Americans were taken aback by this brazen means of intimidation. When Mancos asked how the Chinese were able to secure those names, and so quickly, he was told that very young Chinese boys dressed in drab brown quilted uniforms were paid to infiltrate the NATO troops to bring back pertinent information valuable to the Chinese. The boys noted where the food was stored and ammunition kept, and when the Chinese received this information the mortars began dropping in those very spots. *The Chinese knew everything.*

The Americans slept in makeshift bunkers made of sandbags with hammocks hung as far off the floor as possible as the floor had inches of water standing on it. They slept in a sleeping bag with their clothes on and their .45 caliber gun lying on their chest. They zipped their bag up as close to their chin as they could get it, so the Chinese could not come in and slit their throat during the night. The enemy knew not to attract any attention by shooting someone or by making noises.

The men ate C-rations whenever they had the opportunity, only cherishing a hot meal once in a while. There were no showers and the water in the nearby falls was way too cold for bathing in March. The only option was a sponge bath to get off the thick mud. If a person took a bath in a stream or river he would come out with blood suckers all over him. It was four months before they would get a real hot shower.

Huge rats were everywhere. The Koreans would grab the rats and tie the tail to their belt. Some men could be seen with several of those creatures wiggling around as they hung there – trying to escape from their captor. This seemed so strange to the Americans, but Koreans were extremely poor so they ate rats, cats, and dogs, so very appalling to the troops.

Radio systems seemed to always fail, so a battery operated telephone system was set up with lines to the men within Mancos' unit and to other units. To lay the lines, a huge roll of wire was placed in a jeep; it would unroll as the jeep traveled in the direction the line was needed. Lines were accidentally severed or were intentionally cut by the enemy in order to bring a repairman into harm's way to be killed. As a lineman, Mancos' job was to wait for a call that a phone line was down, then locate the spot where the wires were broken. He could only hope that he could advance toward the broken line and back again, alive.

PFC Mancos with telephone system

I Was There

The line of communication was vital, as the Chinese had the NATO troops surrounded. Before Mancos would go into enemy territory to trace the broken line, flares were discharged lighting up the whole sky, just like daylight. Since the Chinese were everywhere that procedure helped to locate them for Mancos.

His rifleman training from basic training became of more use than his position as lineman. The men were issued rifles, but as time went on and replacements were needed, the men just grabbed anything they found lying around, even a dead man's rifle or machine gun, or a Chinese burp gun.

The Chinese burp gun had very small bullets and would only penetrate a human at close range. The motive for using that type of weapon was to injure, not to kill. They knew that two other men would come to retrieve the injured man to take him back to base camp. That would then remove all three Americans from the front line.

The first assignment for Mancos' unit was to take Old Baldy from the Chinese. First, nine-hundred sixty men from the Columbian Army, a part of NATO Forces, were to take the hill. When Mancos' unit got to the base of the hill, they heard shooting and believed it to be the Columbians.

When the unit advanced the hill they found all the Columbians dead. What the Columbians did not know was that the Chinese had dug a trench seven to eight-hundred yards long. It came up in the middle of the hill where they caught the Columbians off guard and cut their throats or strangled them. The dead were piled up like a cord of wood.

I Was There

Whenever the Chinese attacked, they first blew whistles and horns, rang bells, and shouted. They came in waves like a swarm of ants. First wave would come at the NATO troops, and then the second wave would pick up the guns left by the dead Chinese and carry on the attack. A third wave would follow and try to finish off the attack.

The Chinese would then pull back. After fifteen or twenty minutes, the loud noises would again begin signaling that they were on their way. It was well-known that the Chinese were on drugs making them very aggressive. Mancos describes those attacks "as sitting on an ant hill where you felt very out numbered. As soon as the attack starts, the commotion stopped. Then watch out for mortars."

A look of horror comes on the face of Mike Mancos when he shares the horrific use of very young children by the Chinese and North Korean. Knowing that American's revere life and are very protective of children, they would strap a bomb to the back of a child and send him/her forward to the American lines hoping to destroy lives when it blew up. The children were told that they must carry out this mission or their family would be killed.

Mancos recalls a much lighter episode that he won't ever forget. "One day as I stood near a road I saw an oversized Jeep that was larger than I'd ever seen before and it had huge flags flying from it. Three black people were in the vehicle, which appeared to be two guards and another man. All of a sudden from behind me I heard, 'I say, ole chap, can you tell me where I can find the Ethiopian Army?'"

I Was There

Mancos turned and saw a small black man dressed in a uniform standing there. He looked at the man and then back at the Jeep and said, "Is that Heile Selassie in that Jeep?"

"How do you know him?" asked the guard

"I read about him in my history class in high school."

That brought a smile to the man's face. He ushered Mancos down to the Jeep to meet the Emperor.

"How do you know me?" asked His Highness.

Mancos repeated what he'd told the guard about reading about him in school.

"I came to visit my troops. Can you tell me where I can find them?"

Mancos pointed down the road and to the left. As the oversized-flag-waving jeep drove away, he stood in the road shaking his head in disbelief. *I actually met and talked with Heile Selassie. Well, I'll be!*

The Ethiopians arrived in Korea in June 1951 and did not leave until April 1954. They were a part of the Emperor's Kagnew Battalions sent there as part of the United Nations forces.

The Kagnew Battalions served with great distinction alongside the U.S. 7th Infantry Division. They suffered one hundred twenty-one casualties and over five hundred wounded during the conflict. At the conclusion of the war, the Ethiopians were the only contingent that had *no* prisoners to collect from the North Koreans since no Kagnew soldier ever surrendered. The other distinction was that they never left their dead behind. The Chinese as well as the Koreans had never seen black fighters before, and because of their outstanding record were thought to be super human.

I Was There

PFC Mancos' tour of duty in Korea lasted from March 1953 to July 1954. In his collection of memorabilia, Mancos has a yellowed newspaper clipping from *The Bayonet* – *7th Infantry Division* newspaper dated July 20, 1953. The article is titled "A Message from the Commanding General" and is written by Major General Arthur G. Trudeau, U. S. Army Commander. Excerpts from that article follows:

> *To the men of all ranks in my division and to attached and supporting units: The Bayonet Division has again emerged victorious after violent and sustained combat . . .*
>
> *Let the sacrifices, selflessness, courage and intense devotion to duty rendered by you and your units be a guiding light to all of us in war and in peace. From such understanding of these basic human qualities and values, there is still hope for a revitalized and peaceful world.*
>
> *With price, confidence and renewed determination let us keep our banners high, our weapons clean and our bayonets sharp as long as the superiority of the Bayonet Division is challenged by any foe.*

During the latter months of the war, when an armistice was trying to be signed, the Chinese found every reason to delay the process. When it finally happened, the Chinese blasted over their loud speakers: "Americans, come to our party. Welcome Americans. Celebrate the truce with booze, women and flags." Mancos said, "It was a strange sight observing all the NATO forces, together with Communist Chinese, North and South Koreans partying together and showing family pictures from their wallets to one another."

With the war over, the men were taken to Seoul to catch a flight home. The scene in Seoul was one of complete devastation, no building left untouched. The President's Palace, called the Blue House, had huge holes in it from rockets and bombs. The citizens had built make-shift homes for themselves out of pieces of wood, metal sheets, cardboard, and pieces of cloth or canvas. They had gathered anything they could find from buildings that were either bombed or burned to construct a roof over the heads for their family.

Mancos flew from Seoul's Kimpo International Airport back to Michigan for a thirty-day leave as his dad had just had a stroke. After his leave, PFC Mancos was assigned to the 82nd Airborne at Ft. Bragg, North Carolina. There, at the psychological warfare school, he was taught how to brainwash others, how to accept punishment should he be captured at any time and how to prepare propaganda pamphlets. He stayed at Ft. Bragg until he was discharged in 1955.

He is proud to say that every member of his battalion was given the Bronze Star for their battles in Korea at Old Baldy and Pork Chop Hill. When asked what the military did for him, Mike Mancos says, "It made a man out of me. Woke me up to reality."

For the next year Mike worked for AAA printing pamphlets. He went on from there to beauty school and became a good beautician for the next ten years. He said with a grin, "Beauty school was a great place to find good-

I Was There

looking women." He then dabbled in real estate for twelve years, making quite a bit of money. After that he owned a construction company in Gross Isle, Michigan.

Mike married Wilma in 1957 and the two raised six children – two girls and four boys. In 1968, Mike and two of his sons moved to Panama City where he opened a construction business called Economy Home Repair. The marriage was dissolved at a later date.

Mike is well-known at the Veterans' Home. He is vice-president of the Residents' Council at Sims and acts as a mediator between the residents and the staff in any and all situations.

Mike Mancos is very proud of his four grandsons who have chosen to serve in the military like their grandfather. The last grandson to enter the Army is Ryan, who just enlisted and serves with the 10th Mountain Division. Jacob is a sergeant with the Army Rangers. Anthony is a captain in the Army stationed at Ft. Benning, Georgia. Joseph is an Army Black Hawk pilot who has had tours of duty in Iraq. He became a warrant officer at age nineteen, the youngest helicopter pilot ever.

Ryan   Jacob   Anthony   Joseph.

◄►

I Was There

T/Sgt. Thomas J. Calhoun

was there at Korea's 38th Parallel and in Vietnam

33rd Infantry Division
(Yellow cross on black background)

Thomas Jefferson (T.J.) Calhoun was born in 1930 at Bainbridge, Georgia, a vibrant community of historic homes, many parks and bass fishing in the Flint River. He enlisted in the Army at age eighteen and proceeded immediately to Ft. Jackson, South Carolina for eight weeks of combat training. Then it was on to Panama for jungle training.

The weather was hot, snakes were big and countless monkeys scampered everywhere. Calhoun and the others walked carefully, as the snakes search for water and shelter during the dry season or during brush fires and hide under a pile of leaves or in cracks in a cement wall. Panama's largest venomous snake, the bushmaster, is a pit viper that injects venom through long fangs. In addition to the pit vipers, Panama has some snakes with neurotoxic venom, poison that attacks the central nervous system. As the venom takes effect respiratory failure and cardiac arrest become very real possibilities. It was necessary to step carefully.

While out in jungle training with the 33rd Infantry Division, Calhoun and the other men of Company B did not sleep in sleeping bags, but would find a spot to rest against a tree trunk. That could be very dangerous as there were snakes in that area that dwell in trees. They lie on a limb and strike a person from that position. Using a flashlight at night is imperative to help guide footsteps and preclude stepping on a snake. The men were partially protected by the high-top boots that they wore. The snakes and monkeys look for food anywhere they can find it, so any droppings from a C-ration meal was very inviting to them.

When not training in the jungle, the men lived back at base camp in very nice barracks and ate good food. They ate lots of bananas, as they were quite prevalent. For the eighteen months Calhoun spent in Panama, he also had to pull guard duty along the Panama Canal in conjunction with men from the Navy, Marines and Army. In the darkness of the night any noise coming from within the confines of the canal would cause a guardsman to jump quickly to investigate. They carried M1 rifles and took aim at anything that moved. Calhoun recalls one time while on such duty something fell into the canal and it scared the wits out of him. He investigated but found nothing wrong. It took a while before his heart beat slowed to normal.

Private Calhoun was saddened by the very poor conditions that the Panamanians lived in. He witnessed women that sat on the side of the street selling anything and everything, with the money going to help the poor. He, as well as other U.S. troops, would buy items they didn't want or need; just to help the cause.

It was time for Company B to proceed to the war zone in Korea by way of Hawaii, where additional troops were picked up. Landing in Korea, his company joined the 24th Infantry Division on the 38th parallel.

24th Infantry

They didn't waste time, but immediately headed for the mountains. Their goal was to reach the 38th parallel. The snow was very deep and they had to sleep anywhere they could find a spot. Men died along the way and could not be buried as the ground was frozen. The bodies would freeze and a canvas tarp would be thrown over them.

The weather went from bad to worse; the men had to deal with the cold heavy rain that seemed to continue day and night. The attitude of the men became worse the more it rained.

One day, Calhoun's unit was assigned to fetch C-rations that were stashed farther down the mountain. South Korean troops accompanied the men and they carried back up the mountain as many cases as possible. On the way up they had to hide behind rocks to dodge mortar rounds that were pelted at them from the Chinese, which made their climb back to the top much slower.

On one such trip up the mountain, Calhoun was hit in the right hip and chest with shrapnel, knocking him down. Medics took him back down the mountain for medical attention. He would later receive a purple heart for those injuries.

Purple Heart Medal

Another instance of trouble took place when the men in his company were headed up Pork Chop Hill to take the hill from the Chinese. It was pitch dark outside. Calhoun and his men began the march upward when he spotted through field glasses Chinese crawling along a trench on the other side of a stream at the bottom of the mountain. He ordered his men to keep advancing forward while he went back down to check on his men that were dug-in adjacent to the Chinese.

S/Sgt. Calhoun did not have a radio with him, so he could not call for backup. He crawled to his men and found his buddy, Floyd Taylor and Ogle in the trench. Just then, a concussion grenade hit Calhoun on the side of his face stunning him for a few minutes, but he still did not realize what had happened. He only knew that his men needed help. He continued to pull Ogle out of the trench, but sad to

I Was There

say he was dead. To this day, Ogle is always on the mind of his friend, T. J.

When he got to a radio, Calhoun called in a patrol, which arrived to help retrieve the men and dead bodies. Early the next morning a jeep took Calhoun to company headquarters where he had to give a full report. There, near the headquarters building, Calhoun saw a pile of dead bodies. A sight no one should ever have to see.

S/Sgt. Calhoun stayed in Korea until early 1953 and was elevated to Sergeant First Class (SFC). When his one year assignment was completed he sailed to Japan. As the ship crossed the Sea of Japan Calhoun looked around him at all the men wanting to see who made it out of the war zone, alive. From Japan he was assigned to Ft. Benning, Georgia where he trained others in artillery combat. While stationed there that he met Frances at a dance in Marianne, Georgia a short distance from the post and they were soon married.

Later, from his duty station in Georgia, SFC Calhoun flew to Greenland for a one-year tour of duty in dreadfully cold weather. So cold, that the men's hands froze to the gun when they grabbed ahold of the gun being used for practice shooting. He enjoyed the experience of watching the natives work to catch fish – something quite unique to the Arctic region. They would wade out into the frigid cold water and spear a fish as it swam by.

Calhoun was elevated to a Technical Sergeant and would next spend a tour in Germany before heading to Vietnam in 1969. During his time away, Frances and their young son lived with Calhoun's parents in Alford, Florida.

I Was There

T/Sgt. Calhoun was stationed in Vietnam for one year as platoon sergeant. With machine guns in hand and grenades strapped to their belts, his men would advance on patrol toward the enemy, hunkered behind slow-moving Army tanks. Many on such a patrol were killed.

The men had to walk slowly and carefully to escape stepping on a booby-trap or anti-personnel mines that dotted the landscape. When sniper fire began, men were sent out to investigate and again for any suspected movement. Some returned – others did not.

It was a long year for Calhoun, one that still bombards his mind from time to time, too difficult to talk about. Death was all around him. He said, "In time of war a man does not take one day at a time – only one step at a time."

After that grueling tour of duty in Vietnam, T/Sgt. Calhoun was sent back to Ft. Benning, Georgia where he retired in 1970. He and his family returned to Alford, Florida to work alongside his father-in-law in his carpenter shop.

When asked what the military life did for him, T. J. would say, "Woke me up. When someone tells me to do something now – I do it."

◄►

I Was There

T/Sgt. Claude A. Nelson

was there in **Korea and Vietnam**

Claude Nelson was born in Shady Grove, Florida in 1931. He had quit school at seventeen but was not able to find any work. He did what he knew he needed to do – what he had contemplated for some time - enlist in the Air Force.

Claude took his oath for enlistment on February 24, 1948 and left for Lackland AFB, Texas soon thereafter. He spent fourteen weeks there and then flew to Hamilton Field, Louisiana as an unassigned airman. For a year at Hamilton he cleaned guns on P-51 fighter planes, the forerunner of the F-86. He also trained to be a fireman. Two months after starting training he was sent to Kyushau Island, off the southern coast of Japan. There he trained in fire rescue with the 24th Infantry Division.

I Was There

His training was put to good use when a plane returning from Korea could not make it to the runway. It went down in the water just off the coast of Japan. A flight nurse was there along with Nelson and the other rescuers. He recalls how she bravely pulled one young man with a broken leg to ashore as she swam with one hand. Then back she went for two others who had broken legs and arms.

On another occasion a cargo plane from Korea landed with eighteen casualties aboard. His crew had to use a ladder to let down the stretchers. There were no ambulances, so buses with seats removed were used to take the wounded to the hospital.

Another time a plane on fire landed with its wheels up. The pilot had quickly ejected the canopy so as to get it out of the way in order for him to be rescued. That was traumatic time. Nelson's crew had to always be ready at a moment's notice. There were other instances when damaged planes would come in and spin off the runway.

When the Korean Conflict began in 1950, Nelson was just one month short of going home after his thirty-month tour of duty. The Commanding Officer called a meeting of everyone and said, "Boys, I have an announcement. You're not going home." It was hard to describe the disappointment that ensued.

Even though his grandfather was dying, Nelson could not go home, but was shipped to Korea with his unit. The men lived in ten-man tents with double bunks at a base camp just south of Seoul. The heat and humidity was so atrocious, that it was hard to sleep at night. Nelson's duty as a fireman was on the flight line where he and the crew would extinguish fires of disabled planes that crashed upon

I Was There

landing. During their time in Korea, no one was allowed off base.

In the spring of 1951 A1C Nelson was leaving Korea on a ship headed for Yokohama, Japan. Twenty days later he left there on a plane to San Francisco where he was discharged from the Air Force. He and fifty other men chartered a Trailways Bus and headed east. Nelson got off the bus at eight in the evening, anxious to surprise his family. When he rang the doorbell at his home, his youngest sister, Linda, saw who it was and screamed. His mother came running and when she saw him, she too screamed. She was delight that he was home but also mad that he had not told her he would be arriving. Everyone in the family was there; his dad and sisters Marie, Velia, and Linda along with his brothers Julian and Kenneth.

Clyde did not stay at home long as jobs were so scares. After much contemplation, prayer and discussions with family, he reenlisted in the Air Force. His reenlistment bonus amounted to three-hundred and sixty dollars, far short of today's bonuses. He reported to Ellington Field, a base just outside Houston, Texas where he stayed for six months. The base was used to train Air Force navigators. Then he reported to Foster AFB on the southeast coast of Texas near Victoria. Foster was established as an advanced single-engine flying school for fighter pilots. Nelson was a fireman on the flight line and stayed at that locale for a year-and-a-half.

It was during that time that Nelson got into a fight with another man over a girl. He was taken to the hospital after receiving a cut on the lip and one over his eye. The Air Police were called and he went off to jail. Nelson sweated

I Was There

out the next couple of days while discussions ensued between the Provost Marshall and Nelson's commander as to his punishment. He was then told that the Air Force would not press charges if he would take a reassignment to Big Springs, Texas, near Lubbock. He quickly accepted the assignment. Shortly after Nelson's arrival, the facility was renamed Webb Air Force Base.

At Webb he found out that the infraction from the fist fight back at Foster AFB, which was on his personnel record, had now been cleared. A thankful Nelson could not have been more pleased. Then he was transferred to the 5010th Air Base Group in the fire department at Eielson AFB, Alaska. From the humid heat of Texas to bitterly cold Alaska was quite an adjustment for Nelson.

For thirty months he would hear the B-36 bombers take off with their two jet engines on each wing tip and three prop jet engines, the noise was almost unbearable, and made the windows everywhere rattle.

The weather stayed cold, but things began to warm up when A1C Nelson met Edith a young female first lieutenant. She was in charge of furniture inventory for the base. They dated even though it was forbidden for an officer to date a non-commissioned officer (NCO).

As an NCO, Nelson helped Edith with the Air Force Aid Society (AFAS) to raise money for assisting military families with unexpected financial issues. An example of an emergency assistance issue is AFAS providing travel and incidental expenses to parents when a newborn needs further medical attention at a hospital in the lower forty-eight states.

The pair went to movies on base even though Edith knew it was wrong, and only one person during that time objected. They broke all the rules in the book when they married in February 1955. A chaplain could not perform the ceremony, so they went into town and even though they were not Catholic, asked a priest to perform the ceremony. He agreed. There was standing room only at the wedding; even the base commander was in attendance. Nelson was promoted to S/Sgt. the following month.

Nelson extended his tour of duty at Eielson until the end of his wife's tour of duty, when they were both transferred to Stewart Field, near Newburg, New York. Upon arrival, the Air Force informed Nelson that he would have to be discharged as they had no need of another fireman at that base.

Within days he received notice to be at Base Operations (Base Ops) with bag and baggage. On January 1st, 1957 he had a class assignment at Keesler AFB in Mississippi for air traffic control schooling. Edith had been discharged by then, but stayed at Stewart to await Nelson's return.

I Was There

Nelson received navigational training, landing techniques and meteorology during his time at Keesler. After fourteen months he graduated and returned to Edith and Stewart AFB, where he finished his training. S/Sgt. Nelson loved what he was now doing. It was on-the-job training in the control tower where he knew that concentration and visualization was a vital part of a traffic controller's job.

At the end of that hitch in the Air Force S/Sgt. Nelson decided to get out of the service. But it was only a matter of days before he re-enlisted at Newark, New Jersey at the same rank as when he was discharged. He was assigned to air traffic control at Eglin AFB, Florida. He was pleased to once again return to Florida. With Edith and their three-month-old son, Guy, they moved into in base housing. Nelson was thrilled to be at Eglin, a hop, skip and a jump from his hometown. He remained at Eglin for three years.

In 1961, Nelson's next assignment was to England where he stayed for eighteen months. He became the operator for the control area of American military flights. Edith and their two sons, Guy and Charles, stayed with his parents in Panama City, Florida.

S/Sgt. Nelson's eighteen-month assignment turned into a thirty-month tour of duty due to computer glitch. He was not able to do anything about that error, so he stayed on in England.

The thirty-months passed by slowly, and next, S/Sgt. Nelson was assigned to Tyndall AFB, Florida, a very short distance from his hometown. His assignment was supervisor for air traffic control, which controlled local air traffic, ground traffic and clearances. Ten to twelve jets

I Was There

would leave out each morning from Tyndall for fighter interception training exercises, and it was Nelson's responsibility to assist them with information on visibility, wind direction and altimeter readings. It was an extremely stressful job.

Three years later, S/Sgt. Nelson was on his way to Cameron Bay, Vietnam. When asked what his daily routine consisted of, his reply was, "Work, eat, and sleep." His unit lived in ten-man tents with no air conditioning units. The dining hall was a large tent with only fans being used to keep the men as cool as possible. Cameron Bay had dry heat, and extremely hot weather. Thankfully, the military had provided the men desert uniforms made of material that helped to withstand those high temperatures.

S/Sgt. Nelson was assigned to the radar unit located right next to the runway. There were actually two runways that ran adjacent to each other; one made of cement, the other of Pierced Steel Planking (PSP). They were twelve-foot by six-foot steel mats hooked together to form a runway. His job was to give instructions to pilots of incoming and outgoing planes; F4s, helicopters, and twin-engine C7 cargo planes which looked like gliders with engines affixed to them.

During his time in Vietnam he flew in a C-130 to Clark Air Base in the Philippines. During that flight he was asked to sit in the radio operator's seat, and was thrilled to do so. Upon nearing Clark AB, the rain came down so heavy and hard against the windshield that it was difficult to make out any sign of the runway. The pilot said to those around him, "Keep your eyes open fellas for that strip of concrete where

I Was There

I need to set this baby down." Thankfully, they made it down safe and sound!

After his one-year assignment in Vietnam was completed, Nelson was on a flight back to Florida where he was once again stationed at Tyndall AFB. The family lived in base housing until Claude retired in November 1968. As a civilian he took on many different jobs, not really able to settle into any particular one.

Claude Nelson's wife, Edith, passed away in January 2001. A year later he met Ima Jean Williams while in church and they were soon married. She is the daughter of Asa Williams, a deceased minister of long standing in Panama City, Florida. Ima Jean now resides at a local nursing home.

Claude recently moved to Sims Veterans' Home where he enjoys visits from family and friends.

I Was There

M/Sgt. William J. Peacock, Jr.
was there at a remote
radar site in frigid Alaska

William Peacock was born in Blountstown, Florida in 1930. Twenty-one years later the conflict in Korea had become a full-blown war so he enlisted in the Air Force on June 1, 1951 to avoid being drafted into the Army.

Peacock completed his basic training at Lackland AFB, Texas where he had to live in a tent during the next three weeks. He then traveled by train to Presque, Maine near the Canadian border where he trained to be a meat cutter. For the rest of his military career he worked in central meat cutting plants, processing meat for the military dining halls. He worked in forty-five degree temperatures cutting up the carcasses of beef, pork and lamb and quartering chickens, placing each cut of meat in separate steel pans for delivery to the dining halls.

Corporal Peacock spent 1952-1953 at a remote radar site near McGrath, Alaska, half way between Fairbanks and Elmendorf AFB. It was a twelve-month tour of duty for about one-hundred men and no one could leave the area except for medical emergency during that year.

It was so isolated that one could only get there by means of a bush pilot landing on a dirt runway fifteen miles from the actual radar site. The bulk of supplies for the site was brought in by barges or in a C-47 in the summer and then stored. Mail was received a couple of times a week, in good weather. William operated the mechanical dairy-making machine that makes ice cream. He also managed the warehouse.

In 1953 Sergeant Peacock's year was up in Alaska and he was transferred to Parks AFB in Oakland, California. While on leave from Parks, Peacock went home and married Ruth, and she joined him in California. They lived in an apartment in Hayward, California near the base. He was discharge from the Air Force at Parks, ending his military career, so he thought. One week after arriving back in Florida he was out at Tyndall AFB, Florida re-enlisting.

S/Sgt. Peacock was then transferred to Perrin AFB near Dennison, Texas where he spent the next eight years cutting meat. After that long stint, he was transferred to England. He and Ruth along with daughter, Shirley Ann spent the next three years at Chicksand, thirty miles north of London. Peacock bought a Renault (steering wheel on the left) and they were on the road every weekend touring England.

I Was There

On one such jaunt, they took the ferry across to the European continent where they visited Amsterdam, Rotterdam and Brussels. They loved exploring the many castles and chalets in France and Germany. They family loved every minute that they lived in England.

After three years M/Sgt. Peacock was reassigned to Lackland AFB, where he retired on January 7, 1971. The family moved to Panama City where William was hired at the Tyndall AFB commissary as a meat cutter. He found quite a difference between cutting meat for the military compared with the automated system that the commissary used. Those machines wrapped, sealed, weighed and priced the article of meat, all within minutes. He enjoyed the twenty years there, especially meeting the customers.

Although retired for a second time, Peacock could not just sit still. He drove school buses for the Bay County School District for the next ten years. His route took him to Rutherford High School, Everitt Middle School, and Cherry Street Elementary.

Sadly, Ruth passed away three years ago. His daughter, Shirley, lives in Lynn Haven, a short distance from the Veterans' Home and visits often. His three grandsons and the three great-grandchildren, a boy and two girls also make regular visits.

William Peacock has lived at Sims Veterans' Home for over a year and is pleased to have a good home there.

◄►

I Was There

M/Sgt. Eldon C. Haddock, Jr.
was there in the supply room during
the Korean Conflict and the Vietnam War

Eldon Haddock was born in 1927 at Live Oak, Florida, a small town with a quiet atmosphere. He enlisted in the Air Force in 1947 at Eglin Air Force Base in the Panhandle of Florida. The day he enlisted, he and some of his buddies had been standing around at an Amoco service station in Live Oak a block from Eldon's home, talking about what they planned to do with their lives and where they were going to work.

One friend said, "I ain't gonna work, I'm goin' in the Army." He then turned to me and asked, "Don't you wanna

I Was There

go with me?" I replied, "I don't know. Guess I'll go talk to the recruiter."

It just so happened that the recruiting office was right across the street from that service station in the basement of the post office. Haddock made his way over there and talked with the recruiter for some time, but didn't pay any attention to the uniform he was wearing. After signing the paperwork and believing he was now in the Army, he found out that he was actually in the Air Force. The small town had only one recruiting office for all the services, a fact unknown to Haddock. When asked how his dad took the news, Eldon said, "He was glad as he didn't like the fellas I was hanging around with. I'd become a little on the wild side."

From that small community of Live Oak, Eldon traveled to Lackland AFB in Texas for his basic training and then to technical school in Denver, Colorado followed by a year in El Paso, Texas and Shreveport, Louisiana. Haddock was then given an overseas assignment. He was sent to Kadena Air Base near Tokyo, Japan, where he was stationed for two years during the Korean Conflict. He was put in charge of supplies running the gamut from soup to nuts, ammunition to clothing. Not only were they stored there, but supplies had to be dispersed, ordered when a request came in, inventoried, and back-ordered when necessary.

In his modesty, Haddock feels that his duties were not as significant as those of the men and women who fought on the front lines during war time. But, if truth be told – HAD NOT clothing, food, guns, ammunition and medical supplies been provided to those in the thick of war they would have been in a world of hurt.

Being in a supply unit, his job during his two-year stint in Japan, was to keep the supplies flowing continually to the war zone in Korea. Haddock said, "As with any military unit, when someone wants an item from the supply room, they want it NOW and that is a supply supervisor's biggest headache."

Upon his departure from Japan, he was stationed at Holloman AFB near Alamogordo, New Mexico. His time there was well spent with his job but also that is where he met Agnes. Haddock and some of the men from his unit would go to Ruidoso, New Mexico, a resort area, hoping to meet girls. And that is where Agnes worked. The two met and dated for a short while before being married.

S/Sgt. Haddock stayed at Holloman AFB for two years, just long enough for two children to be born. Then orders were handed to him for an American base in Morocco. Although he left without his family, several months later Agnes and the two babies joined him there. Military housing was in the process of being built at that time, so the family lived in an apartment downtown over a bakery.

Soon, a three-bedroom house on the base was completed and the family moved in. He was promoted to master sergeant and Morocco would become the longest duty station for him – four years. The country was centrally and strategically located for the military, so his job was to send supplies to military installations in Germany, France, North Africa and many other countries. M/Sgt. Haddock worked with a crew of men plus twenty Frenchmen in the supply warehouse.

The Haddock family loved their time in Morocco, especially the weather, even though it was hot – very hot. He purchased a '41 Ford pickup which they used to tour the area, sightseeing and picking grapes which were quite prevalent in the area. Morocco was still under the influence of France at that time, only securing its independence on March 2, 1956, shortly after the Haddocks left.

In the next few years, the Haddocks saw a lot of the United States on assignments that took the family to Portsmouth, New Hampshire, where a son was born nearby at Kittery, Maine. From there it was on to Jackson, Michigan where he became an Air Force recruiter. Then it was back to a warehouse supervisor's position in Charleston, South Carolina.

M/Sgt. Haddock's next assignment took him away from the family and the U.S. He was assigned to the supply warehouse at headquarters in Saigon, Vietnam for one year during the war. No attacks happened on the grounds of the headquarters, but continual bombardment of explosions could be heard and the ground shook. He emphasized that the Americans were treated quite well by the Vietnamese – after all "we were money to them." He returned to Agnes and the children, stationed in New Jersey where he retired at age forty-seven.

After retirement, Mr. Haddock spent time doing volunteer work for the VFW. Friends they had known in the Air Force invited the couple to visit them in Panama City, Florida. Eldon really wanted to live in Florida as, after all, his birthplace was Live Oak, Florida, a small town halfway between Tallahassee and Jacksonville. So, the family moved there. Eldon and Agnes ran a plant nursery for several years in Panama City and he even tried his hand at mediating at the court house.

In 1998 cancer tragically took the life of their eldest daughter. And just a few years ago, the neuropathy in Eldon's legs caused them to become very weak. One day he tried to walk to the bathroom and his legs went out from under him and he broke his neck in the fall. He is quite a large man; Agnes stands only five feet tall and could not take care of him after that accident. Since then he has lived at Sims Veterans' Home where he gets the care he needs.

The white-bearded gentleman, who could pass for Santa Claus, spends his time wheeling around the Veterans' Home in a wheelchair visiting with other residents. Haddock joins in with men in the activity room where a staff member reads the newspaper and later they have a time of exercise. He enjoys visits from his wife and children who dearly love him. He proudly boasts that he has nine grandchildren and twenty-three great-grandchildren who also adore him.

◀▶

I Was There

I Was There

Corporal Earl G. Spence
was there in Germany

Earl Spence was born in 1932 in Mineola, Long Island, New York. Mineola is a Native American word meaning a "pleasant place." He enlisted in the Army in 1949 at Ft. Dix, New Jersey at age seventeen. After his training was completed he had orders for Korea as an infantryman. Soon after his arrival there he was injured and that is also when the military discovered he was only seventeen years old. The cutoff age for combat duty is eighteen. He was quickly removed from Korea.

In 1950, Spence had orders for Nuremburg, German again as an infantryman. It had only been a few short years since the end of World War II, but Nuremburg still looked like a war zone. Fifty percent of the city was still in ruins and the people remained in a depressed state of mind. Train service, which is Germany's main means of transportation, had just been revived when Spence arrived there.

His company was sent to the German/Russian border to stand as sentries against any move toward an invasion into Germany. The two armies stood on each side of the border staring at each other. Many of the Russian soldiers were just boys, maybe sixteen or seventeen years of age. During the winter, they along with the Americans enjoyed a time of throwing snowballs at each other across the border.

During his tour of duty in Germany Private First Class (PFC) Spence met Elise, a pretty young Germany lady. She lived on a farm with her mother and step-father. The farm had been untouched by the bombings during World War II. Members of her family were quite impressed with Spence's interest in learning German and he soon became their adopted son. In 1955, Spence and Elise married and in 1957 their first child was born – a girl, Leisel.

Spence's new father-in-law had been a German soldier caught by the Americans and held at Mitchell Field on Long Island as a prisoner-of-war. Since Spence was from Long Island and could now speak German the two spent a great deal of time talking about the elder man's incarceration.

PFC Spence's prolific use of the Germany language was put to good use by the Army as an interpreter. Because he spoke Deutsch (low Bavarian) so well, he could interpret whenever needed, such as for a car accident that might happen between an American and a German.

In 1957, he had orders to return to the States, but at the last minute they were canceled and his tour extended to eight more months in Germany. He had already sent his wife and daughter on to New York to stay with his parents when this happened. The extension came due to President Truman and the Pentagon's concern that the Russians might penetrate Germany. At the end of the eight months Corporal Spence returned to Ft. Dix where he received his discharge papers.

Since Earl loved construction work, his first job after being discharged was with a company that built houses. That only lasted a while until he started his own milk route delivering glass bottled milk and other dairy products. He collected the milk in large milk cans from the farmers and transported them to a plant where it was pasteurized and homogenized. He also had four milk routes with four delivery men to oversee. He was the standby driver for anyone who had a day off or was ill.

The winter snow and ice posed a real problem for the delivery routes and so Earl decided to move his family to Montgomery, Alabama where his aunt and uncle lived. He bought up five milk routes and began his new delivery service.

Elise and Earl divorced and in 1987 he moved to Panama City, Florida. He had driven there many times while living in Alabama to swim in the beautiful emerald Gulf waters. Later, he married and again began a delivery route with dairy products.

Earl Spence is the father of five girls; Leisel, Amy, Lori, Bonnie and Susan. He had so wished for a boy, but is delighted with his girls.

◄►

I Was There

I Was There

Korean Conflict Timeline

Aug. 1945: Korea divided into US and Soviet Occupation Zones along 38th parallel

Jun 1950: N. Korean People's Army invades S. Korea

Jun 1950: N. Korea attacks Seoul airfield

Jun 1950: N. Korean army captures Seoul

Jul 1950: US troops fight for the first time – heavy casualties

Jul 1950: US aircraft destroy key oil refinery

Jul 1950: Battle for Taejon ends – heavy US losses

Aug 1950: First UN counterattack collapses

Sep 1950: Inchon landing of UN forces

Sep 1950: UN troops complete recapture of Seoul

Oct 1950: UN forces cross 38th parallel

Oct 1950: Chinese Communist troops cross Yalu River into Korea

Oct 1950: UN captures Pyongyang, N. Korean capital

Nov 1950: Chinese attack in force near Unsan

Nov 1950: Gen. MacArthur's "Home by Christmas" offensive begins

Jan 1951: Seoul captured by Chinese

Jan 1951: UN forces resume offensive

I Was There

Korean Conflict timeline continued:

Feb 1951: Chinese counteroffensive begins

Mar 1951: UN line reaches between 37th and 38th parallels

Mar 1951: UN forces retake Seoul

Apr 1951: MacArthur recalled – Gen. Ridgway takes command

Jun 1951: UN forces dig in on the 38th parallel

Jul 1951: Truce talks begin – Communists break off talks six weeks later

Sep 1951: UN forces take Heartbreak Ridge after 18-day battle

Nov 1951: Truce talks resume at Panmunjom

Mar 1953: N. Korean and Chinese agree to POW exchange

Apr 1953: Three-day battle of Pork Chop Hill ends in victory for UN forces

Apr 1953: Full peace talks resume at Panmunjom

Jun 1953: Communist offensive pushes Republic of Korea troops south

Jun 1953: Chinese launch massive attacks against S. Korean divisions

Jul 1953: Communists return to negotiations

Jul 1953: Cease fire signed – fighting ends 12 hours later

A Salute to
Women in the Military

Women's Army Corps (WACS)

American men were not the only ones jolted by the harsh reality of war. On July 20, 1942, the first female volunteers began their training at Fort Des Moines, Iowa as the Women's Army Auxiliary Corps. Later, the Women's Army Corps (WACs) was established in 1943.

In 1941, public opinion had become increasingly in favor of some role for women in the military, to step into the shoes of men needed on the battlefield. Congress debated the issue with opposition coming from one southern congressman who asked, "Who'll do the cookin', washin' and mendin' to which every women has devoted herself to do?" The bill was approved in May 1941.

I Was There

Members of the press were also skeptics and made a hay-day out of this new American *oddity*, with remarks like, "Can they wear makeup?", and even made claims that the birth rate of our nation would be negatively affected.

Women applicants had to be between twenty-one and forty-five years of age and a U.S. citizen. They had to be at least five feet tall and weight one-hundred pounds or more. More than one-hundred-fifty-thousand women served in World War II doing everything from repairing trucks to making aerial surveys.

The women were not pampered as might be thought by skeptics. They sweated through gas-mask drills and were drenched by rain during long hikes. They had to endure no shades on the barrack's windows and even inspection of their hairdos and the straightness of their stocking seams.

WAVES

Women Accepted for Volunteer Emergency Service

The WAVES organization during World War I had been deactivated. But with the advent of World War II there were a vast number of women who sought to enlist in the Navy. The government had to act quickly to secure individuals to manage recruitment, set up training establishments and design uniforms. Within a year twenty-seven thousand women wore the WAVE uniform.

I Was There

During WWII, women served in a greater capacity than those during WWI. Back then they held down secretarial and nurse positions. But in 1942 they had duties in the fields of aviation, Judge Advocate General Corps, medicine, science and technology.

———

Women Marines
Marine Corps Women's Reserve
Lady Leathernecks

Women in the Marine Corps were organized on February 13, 1943. They were authorized to hold a position in one-hundred fifty jobs, with the same rank and pay as their male counterpart. No formal indoctrination or schooling was provided. They went on active duty immediately.

Among the jobs they performed were radio operator, photographer, parachute rigger, driver, aerial gunnery instructor, cryptographer, auto mechanic and agriculturist.

———

Clifford C. Sims State Veterans' Home is home to several women who proudly served in the U.S. military.

◄►

I Was There

Petty Officer
Sarah C. (Culpepper) Snow
was there in the navy's photo lab
making recruiting films

Sarah Culpepper graduated from a Marianna, Florida high school in 1954. Soon after, she joined the Navy, taking her oath in Dothan, Alabama. This was in peace time - not quite a year after the conflict ended in Korea. She chose the Navy after checking out the plus and minuses of each military service. When she tested, the recruiter told her she had the highest IQ that he had ever seen at that recruiting station.

Her basic training took place at Bainbridge, Maryland where she was appointed as Recruit Chief Petty Officer with the 33rd Company, which carried the responsibility of

I Was There

taking care of the men and women in her company. She did her best to solve whatever problem the recruits had.

Next, she was stationed in Jacksonville, Florida where she attended the Aviation Fundamental School. This move was questionable for Sarah, as women were not allowed to fly with the Navy at that time. She studied aviation, but would never use that information.

After a year she was transferred to Pensacola, Florida to the Photography School. She loved the photo lab and earned the rank of Second Class Photographer. She helped produce recruiting films for the Navy, and was fortunate enough to be one of the players in a film. She was thrilled to be station there, as Pensacola has beautiful beaches along the Gulf of Mexico.

The commanding officer of her company was John Philip Sousa, III. Yes, you heard right – John Philip Sousa III. Sarah became acquainted with his wife and ultimately was asked to babysit their two children. She has high praises for that family.

While in Pensacola she had the privilege of going aboard the carriers Enterprise and Lexington and that opportunity is a fond memory of hers today. She was awed by the size of the ships and also the number of men and planes each ship carried. "It was like a floating city," she said.

After a year, Culpepper was transferred to Corpus Christi, Texas where she was once again assigned to a photo lab, where she developed and framed pictures. She loved the Navy. As a people-person, that life gave her the chance to meet many people.

I Was There

The WAVE barracks was across the street from the barracks which housed the Navy Cadets learning to fly. At that time, those officers were not allowed to date non-commissioned officers – but they did. Those men were the only ones Culpepper dated until she met a man who she fell madly in love with. He also worked in the photo lab and they married in June 1957 when she was twenty-one years old.

Culpepper completed her three-year hitch and was discharged in 1957. Just prior to her discharge she was selected to attend Officers Candidate School (OCS), but turned the opportunity down, choosing instead to be a stay-at-home mom and tend to the man she loved. One year later the marriage ended, leaving Sarah devastated. She took little Melissa and made her way back home to Florida.

Sarah lived with her parents on their farm in Marianna, Florida, and it was there that she began to pick up the pieces of her life. She soon secured a job as legal secretary in the law office of Dewey Johnson and his partner, Tracy Riddle in the small community of Quincy, Florida.

While employed there she lived with her grandmother in Quincy and also took care of Melissa while Sarah worked. Sarah describes her grandmother as a 'real hoot'.

She became politically active while working for Mr. Johnson, who was deeply imbedded in politics. During Sarah's employment at the law office, Mr. Johnson ran for political office becoming the Democratic Senator from that district, and in 1959 became the President of the Florida Senate. Sarah's deep interest in politics began there and continues to this day.

I Was There

In 1961, Sarah married Marvin Carlson and moved to Tallahassee. They had a son, James Carlson. She worked in the personnel department for the State of Florida Department of Agriculture. Her work in personnel was the perfect job for Sarah, who calls herself a 'real people person'. Marvin passed away and she was once again left alone, this time with two children.

In 1969, Sarah met and married Robert G. Snow, an Electrical Engineer/Design Engineer for power plants. Their home was in Greensboro, Florida, a town so small it only has one traffic signal. They were married for thirty years – "good years," Sarah exclaims. His engineering position took him to other states; Massachusetts, South Carolina and Texas to build atomic plants. Sarah and the children moved right along with him. He retired at the end of that hitch in the Air Force.

Robert suddenly upped and left one day and when he did Sarah moved to Panama City, Florida where her long-time good friend lived. She resided at the St. Andrew Towers a senior-citizens high-rise apartment that overlooks St. Andrew Bay. She occupied her time with friends, going out to lunch and enjoyed a good game of bridge.

Sarah attributes her good work ethic to her three-year hitch in the navy where she matured and excelled. She would not trade her experiences in the navy for anything else.

She has lived at the Sims Veterans' Home for three years – and is quite appreciative of the opportunity to have such a good place to reside during her senior years.

I Was There

Airman Second Class
Hazel B. (Bostick) Getkin
was there in the Diet Kitchen

Hazel Bostick was born in 1929 in Potsdale, New York and after graduating high school she attended St. Lawrence University. That is also where actor Kirk Douglas and FOX news reporter, Martha MacCallum, attended.

In 1957 Hazel decided to join the Air Force, hoping to make a career of it. When asked why she chose the Air Force over the other services, she said, "I like the color blue." Guess it's as good a reason as any.

She took her basic at Lackland AFB, Texas. Next came technical school at Chanute Field, Illinois where she attended classes for becoming a dietician. She learned to prepare meals and make menus. She returned to Lackland for two years, where she worked in the hospital's dietary unit.

In her spare time at Chanute she instituted a woman's drill team of twenty to thirty active duty women. They marched in parades, change of command ceremonies and all kinds of activities.

One parade she vividly remembers is the time *her girls* marched down State Street in Chicago. It was a miserably cold day – and true to form for Chicago the wind was blowing up a storm. The girls wore their winter uniform that day with long sleeved t-shirts underneath to help keep them warm – thankfully, they had on slacks.

When Hazel was asked if her supervisor disliked the amount of time she spent away from the job on the days the girls marched, she said, "Not at all. Lieutenant Driggs always encouraged me and attended main of our outings."

A2C Bostick met Robert Getkin a Technical Sergeant who worked in the same hospital's mess hall. He was a cook. A short time later they were married.

Two years later Hazel bore a daughter, Louanne and then thirteen months after that a son, Michael, was born.

With the added responsibility of motherhood, Hazel sought a discharged at the end of her hitch. Robert went on to retire several years later.

T/Sgt. Getkin was transferred to Tyndall AFB, Florida where he worked in the hospital's kitchen. They had met many friends while stationed at Tyndall and decided that they would retire in Panama City.

After his retirement, Robert continued to work at Tyndall as a civilian in one of the mess halls.

I Was There

Hazel is a spunky individual who wheels herself up and down the halls of the Veterans' Home. She feels very thankful for the opportunity to live there and receive the kind of medical attention she needs.

◄►

I Was There

Vietnam Era Veterans' Stories

Vietnam Memorial in Washington D.C.

I Was There

S/Sgt. Clifford Chester Sims

was there in South Vietnam
in 1968

The *Clifford Chester Sims State Veterans' Home* in Panama City, Florida was named for Staff Sergeant (S/Sgt.) Sims, a Medal of Honor recipient.

He was born in Port St. Joe, Florida on June 18, 1942 and entered the regular army in Jacksonville, Florida in a Military Occupational Specialty code (MOS) as 11B4P.

Twenty-five year old Sims was killed on February 21, 1968, while serving as a squad leader with Company D, 2d Battalion (Airborne), 501st Infantry, 101st Airborne Division near Hue, Thua Thien province of South Vietnam. (See the citation for his Medal of Honor on the next page.) S/Sgt. Sims was buried in Barrancos National Cemetery, Pensacola, Florida.

In a formal ceremony, U.S. Vice President Spiro Agnew presented S/Sgt. Sims' wife her husband's Medal of Honor posthumously.

S/Sgt. Sims' name is on the Vietnam wall in Washington D.C. at panel 40E, row 056.

S/Sgt. Sims' Medal of Honor Citation

For conspicuous gallantry and intrepidity in action at the risk of his life above and beyond the call of duty, S/Sgt. Sims distinguished himself while *serving as a squad leader with Company D. Company D was assaulting a heavily fortified enemy position concealed within a dense wooded area when it encountered strong enemy defensive fire. Once within the woodline, S/Sgt. Led his squad in a furious attack against an enemy force which had pinned down the 1st Platoon and threatened to overrun it. His skillful leadership provided the platoon with freedom of movement and enabled it to regain the initiative. S/Sgt. Sims was then ordered to move his squad to a position where he could provide covering fire for the company command group and to link up with the 3rd Platoon, which was under heavy enemy pressure. After moving no more than 30 meters, S/Sgt. Sims noticed that a brick structure in which ammunition was stocked was on fire. Realizing the danger, S/Sgt. Sims took immediate action to move his squad from this position. Though in the process of leaving the area 2 members of his squad were injured by the subsequent explosion of the ammunition, S/Sgt. Sims' prompt actions undoubtedly prevented more serious casualties from occurring. While continuing through the dense woods amidst heavy enemy fire, S/Sgt. and his squad were approaching a bunker when they heard the unmistakable noise of a concealed booby trap being triggered immediately to their front. S/Sgt. Sims warned his comrades of the danger and unhesitatingly hurled himself upon the device as it exploded, taking the full impact of the blast. In so protecting his fellow soldiers, he* *willingly sacrificed his life. S/Sgt. Sims' extraordinary heroism at the cost of his life is in keeping with the highest traditions of the military service and reflects great credit upon himself and the U.S. Army.*

The Florida Department of Veterans' Affairs and the family of Clifford C. Sims named the lovely veterans facility in honor of him.

I Was There

T/Sgt. Clyde L. Phelps
was there in Vietnam
53 months with Red Horse

When Clyde Phelps was born on July 31, 1939, hardly anyone had heard of a country called Vietnam. But some twenty plus years later Clyde would find himself in the rice paddies of that *now* well-known country.

Clyde Phelps grew up in Lakeland a beautiful city in the northern part of the Florida peninsula. His dad had been a Seabee and his two brothers were in the Navy, so he joined the Air Force in 1958 – just to be different.

His first assignment was at Seymour Johnson AFB, North Carolina. In 1959 he was sent to Keplavik., Iceland. It was there that Airman Phelps saw snow for the first time and darkness for the greater part of each day.

I Was There

The American military was sent there to furnish protection for the Icelanders. Phelps found the local natives to be non-violent and lived a life of austerity, similar to an Amish community. The economy was driven by fish they caught daily.

For thirteen months, Airman Phelps worked in the motor pool where he drove a school bus for the military dependent children. He picked up the children on his route and then drove them to the Navy chow hall for breakfast and again at lunch time. With each trip he counted noses to make sure that every child was accounted for.

While the children were in school he gassed up the bus and washed it among other assignments given him for the day. Making friends with the kids and their families was the greatest joy in his tour of duty in Iceland. He was promoted at Keflavik to Airman Second Class (A2C).

The next assignment for A2C Phelps brought him to Yokota, Japan with the 513th field Maintenance Squadron. His section of that squadron was called Arial Space Ground Equipment to support the planes based there.

His unit refueled fighter jets as well as KB-29s, often referred to as *a thousand nuts and bolts flying in loose formation*. He spent three years and four months at Yokota, and during that time promoted to Airman First Class (A1C)

While stationed in Yokota, Japan in 1965, his unit had to be ready to be shipped anywhere in the world at any moment and a 'Go Bag' needed to be packed. That bag consisted of an up-to-date shot record, .30 caliber carbine, and one hundred rounds of ammunition.

One day he was told he was to be ready to leave – but this time in civilian clothes. Sixty-seven men were handed

I Was There

one hundred dollars each and told to board the C-46 Commando Carbine awaiting them on the tarmac. As they walked to the plane it was so clearly obvious that no writing was on its side.

When the plane was loaded, the pilot, also in civilian clothes, took the plane out on the runway. Not a word was said to the passengers as to where they were going. Thirty minutes later with the flaps down the plane landed at Epsusga Naval Air Station. The men got off and were directed to a Quonset nut were they were briefed by a full bird colonel and then they were back on the plane at daylight. Still the men did not have the slightest inkling as to where they were going.

Since it was a cargo plane there were very few windows, but as darkness permeated the inside of the plane, the flaps going down could be heard and then the landing gear. The men looked at each other wondering *where are we now?*

One man went to a window and could see the words *Bangkok, Thailand Airport* on the side of the terminal. When the plane landed it did not stop at the terminal but continued on to the end of the taxiway, pulling up on the grass.

A Thai captain met them as the men deplaned. They were actually at the Royal Thai Air Force Base. For the next seven months the assignment called for the men to continue wearing civilian clothes. The details of their time there cannot be told.

Returning to Yokota Air Base A1C Phelps submitted his 'dream list' for bases where he next wanted to be stationed. They included:

I Was There

Homestead AFB in Florida
Patrick AFB in Florida
Barksdale AFB in Louisiana
Huma AFB in Louisiana
Hunter AFB in Savannah, Georgia.
All close to his home in Florida.

As happens in so many cases, he was not given any one of those bases. Instead, his orders assigned him to a Strategic Air Command (SAC) base near Plattsburgh, New York – fifteen miles south of the Canadian border. This southern boy was not too pleased. He knew he was in for some mighty cold winters.

A1C Phelps was assigned to the Organized Maintenance Squadron (OMS). They towed aircraft – the old KC97s and B47s that were then moth-balled, replaced by the first generation of KC135s and B52s.

It was there in Plattsburg that an unusual assignment presented itself. Men from four different Air Force bases: Ramsey in Puerto Rico, Plattsburg in New York, Pine in Oregon, and Travis in California, were hand picked at random to go to Vietnam. Those men were of varied working skills on a mission to Tan Son Nhut, South Vietnam for one hundred fifty days.

They were given a set of blueprints and asked, "Can you do this?" Men who were not carpenters or handy men were asked to pour the foundation and build a metal building to specifications.

The reason: to see if Prime Beef (Base Engineer Emergency Force) could construct such a building in a short period of time. Prime Beef lacked heavy equipment and skills, so could they respond to a call for supplemental support in the event of bomb damage or disasters? The war called for quick repairs and replacements of buildings and this test would give the engineers the answer to that question.

Prime Beef finished the project early -- in one-hundred twenty days. The building was accepted after being processed through several levels of quality control inspection – the first time around. The men wanted to go home, but had to wait for others to complete their mission. The men returned to their units proud of their efforts.

Prime Beef having passed the Air Force's test it was now tagged suitable for the kind of work needed in Vietnam and other war zones. The squadrons formed were called RED HORSE (RH) (Rapid Engineer Deployable Heavy Operational Repair Squadron Engineers). The first two squadrons were the 554th (Penny Short) and the 555th (Triple Nickel). They were both deployed to Southeast Asia in November 1965.

Rapid Engineer Deployable Heavy Operational Repair
Squadron Engineers (RED HORSE)[2]

---

[2] Phelps at Red Horse 35th anniversary of excellence, Hurlburt Field, Florida in 2000.

I Was There

In 1966, Phelps was sent from Plattsburgh on another TDY set of orders to Vietnam with Red Horse's 554th. He was shortly thereafter sent back to the States to Edwards AFB where he spent six months in schooling on operating one-hundred ton cranes. Those cranes would be needed in Vietnam to build runways and parking ways for the planes.

He returned to Vietnam in 1966 assigned to Red Horse with the 823rd, Detachment 1 as a heavy equipment operator. That detachment built steel buildings and laid Pierced Steel Planking (PSP) for temporary runways.

Phelps remained in Vietnam until 1970.

While there in 1969, Phelps began to experience physical oddities. His hair began to fall out along with his eye lashes and infamous mustache. He didn't understand what was happening to him. It wouldn't be until 1975 that he would hear the diagnosis of being contaminated with Agent Orange.

———————

According to the website: www.publichealth.va.gov, Agent Orange was part of the United States' strategy in Vietnam to remove foliage that provided cover for the enemy. The herbicide was made up of two ingredients:

- 2,4-dichlorophenoxyacetic acid (2,4-D)
- 2,4,5-trichlorophenoxyacetic acid (2,4,5-T), Containing minute traces of 2,3,7,8-tetra-chiodibenzo-p-dioxin.

I Was There

The pesticide was known to cause a variety of illnesses in laboratory animals.

The name "Agent Orange" came from the orange stripe used on the 55-gallon drums in which it was stored. The chemical itself was the color orange like that of Tang®.

Military planes were used to spray the 2,4,5 pesticide over the foliage causing it to die. That compound was the first to be used. It was mixed with water. When men came in contact with it, it could be easily blown off the skin as the water would have evaporated immediately in the extreme heat of Vietnam leaving only the powder. But later, when diesel fuel was added to make 2,4,5D the pesticide would not dissolve, but adhere to the skin.

During 1961 through 1971, more than nineteen million gallons of various herbicides were sprayed in Vietnam, with Agent Orange used most often. Areas that were heavily sprayed included the many inland forests of Vietnam but also the forests at the junction of the borders of Cambodia, Laos and South Vietnam.

Those exposed to the pesticide have experienced health problems that include:

- Nervous system
- Rare disease caused when an abnormal protein, amyloid, enters tissues or organs
- Skin condition like that of acne
- Types of cancers
- High blood sugar levels
- Malignant lymphoma
- A disorder characterized by liver dysfunction

- Cancer of the prostate, lungs, larynx, trachea and bronchus.

———————

In 1974, Phelps met Margaret in Manchester, England while stationed there. Amid her parent's objection of an American military man marrying their daughter, the two married in 1975. It was also in 1975, while taking a physical at Chanute AFB, as part of the next step up to the rank of Master Sergeant, the diagnosis of Agent Orange was proclaimed.

Within four months his gums began to bled – so his teeth were pulled. He lost hearing in both ears. Next he experienced heart seizures and two strokes along with kidney failure and acute diabetes. Sergeant Phelps was medically discharged in October 1978. He had spent twenty years in the Air Force.

Upon retirement he entered college to begin studying for an Elementary Education degree. It wasn't until 2000, after a complete medical exam by a female doctor in Biloxi, Mississippi, that he was official pronounced to have Agent Orange. He was approved for one hundred percent disabled for combat related Agent Orange.

Soon a long list of diseases and physical problems developed to include strokes as the result of Agent Orange. Clyde Phelps had to have additional daily assistance, so he entered the Sims Veterans' Home. Margaret, his loving wife, who lives nearby visits Clyde quite often. They sometimes leave the compound to enjoy a meal at a local restaurant.

I Was There

Phelps spends his time as the Resident Librarian at the Veterans' Home making sure that good reading material is accessible for the many veterans residing at Sims. The library has a peaceful atmosphere with beautiful tapestry chairs, a place where the residents can spend time reading away from their rooms. The library is filled with references books about all the wars going back to the Civil War.

◄►

I Was There

I Was There

Machinist Mate III Class
Richard W. Fuller
was there in **Antarctica**

Antarctica Ribbon

Richard Fuller was born in 1946 in San Diego, California, to an Air Force father and a Navy mother. His father passed away in 1963 when Richard was seventeen. When he graduated from high school in 1965, there were very few jobs available and the draft had been instituted for the Vietnam War. So, Richard decided to follow his parent's footsteps and join the military. He chose the Navy, preferring the Air Force, but their quota was full at the time.

On August 1, 1965 Seaman Recruit Fuller headed for the Great Lakes Naval Training Center near Chicago believing he would be trained as an aircraft electrician after graduation from boot camp. But like what so often happens in the military, plans got changed. He was sent to Jacksonville, Florida with orders to become an Aviation Boatswain's Mate as a handler. That training comprised of learning to load and unload cargo onto aircraft.

Soon thereafter, he was transferred to Davisville, Rhode Island, a Seabee base where he was reassigned to the

I Was There

Antarctica Support Activities Unit. He had to attend four different schools before he was able to be stationed in the Antarctic. First was the firefighting school in Tennessee. Then on to Lake Hurst, New Jersey where he studied refueling aircraft. Next came a period of time at Richmond, Virginia to learn about shipboard firefighting. Lastly, he was sent to Marinette, Wisconsin to learn how to fight fires with dry chemicals. The schooling there was extremely important as in the Antarctic fires cannot be fought with water because it freezes as it comes out of the fire hose.

In October 1966, Fuller was on his way to McMurdo in the Antarctica on a Navy C-130. It touched down using skids on the snow-packed runway in forty-five degrees *below* zero weather. He would be there as Navy support to the scientists stationed there. The men were stationed in the Antarctic on temporary duty (TDY) seven months at a time and then reverted back to the States; to return again in seven months.

———

4/1/11 – at this writing the temperature in McMurdo was recorded at -58°F. The night temperature would fall to -71°F, with a chance of snow. Brrrr! Double Brrr!

———

Antarctica covers over five million square miles of unspoiled environment. More than six-hundred researchers have been sent to McMurdo, Antarctica to study microbes that live in extreme cold and also to examine layers of ice tens of thousands of years old.

I Was There

Preparing to leave for Antarctica, Fuller had thoughts running through his head about seeing Mt. Erebus, which is located on Ross Island. It is the southernmost historically active volcano on earth and he had seen pictures of the volcano when he studied about it in high school. Now he would to see it for real. Polar explorer Sir James Clark Ross discovered the twelve thousand four-hundred eighty-eight foot Mt. Erebus in 1841, during one of its eruptions.

Mt. Erebus, Antarctica with smoke still rising from it.

Another lingering desire for Fuller was to see the preserved hut that Captain Robert Falcon Scott had lived in during his expedition to the frozen wilderness in 1912. Scott had led an expedition of five men to the South Pole. A great disappointment met Scott there, when he found out that he had been preceded by Roald Amundsen, a Norwegian explorer. On the return trip to McMurdo, Scott and his four comrades all perished from exhaustion, starvation and extreme cold only many miles from their final destination. Scott was forty-three years old.

Fuller's desire to see Scott's sealed-off twenty-by-twenty foot hut in McMurdo came to fruition. It had been

I Was There

left just as it was back in 1912. Disappointed that he could only look through the windows, he could still see dishes and loose tobacco that remained on the table and the shelves were full of canned goods.

———

While Fuller and the other men worked outside at Williams Field, they wore long Johns covered by leggings and topped with fatigue pants. An insulated parka completed the outfit. Mukluk gloves were worn over the top of another pair of gloves; the outer ones removed to do intricate work, but only for short periods of time. Bare hands would have instantly frozen if touching a cold pipe. A doctor and medical clinic were available to the men at Williams Field and another in-town at McMurdo. Frost bite was probably the most treated ailment at both places.

The sun shone twenty-four hours a day, so the men had to wear sunglasses to shade their eyes from the horrific glare off the ice. Fuller was amazed to discover that there in frozen Antarctica, the sun made a small orbit above the earth four times a day.

Williams Field where the men worked and lived was ten miles from the city of McMurdo. The small crew lived in a Quonset hut that was insulted but still the temperature inside would go down to 40°F at night. While they slept, snow drifted in through the cracks in the building, piling up under their cots.

The huge fire truck that Fuller's crew worked on was called Fire Boss which was a track vehicle with rubber treads and powered by diesel fuel. Fire Boss contained a very large two-thousand pound cylinder that carried the chemicals needed to put out a jet fuel fire or an electrical fire. Each type of fire needed different chemicals to extinguish that fire. The trucks were kept running twenty-four hours a day, so that if they were needed they would be ready to go, as the cold weather could impede a vehicle from starting. The fire department could not take that chance.

Three men manned Fire Boss, a crew-chief, hose man, and the driver who stayed with the truck at all times while on an emergency. The fire truck was always on scene whenever aircraft came in for a landing. Those planes were mostly ones that brought in supplies that had to last for a long stretch of time.

One time, while on the way to the flight line (which was a long strip of glacier ice) the snow came down so hard and thick in a white-out condition that the driver could not see where he was going. The hose man got out to walk in front of Fire Boss and directed the driver by radio. He could only tell where he was going by watching for the black flags posted on both sides of the road. The white-out became worse by the moment and the hose man lost his way and accidently walked onto the runway, with the Fire boss following behind him. The C-130 came in for a landing right over the top of the fire truck. The runway was short and the Fire Boss crew held their breath, afraid that the plane would crash. But, thankfully, it stopped within a thousand feet of the end of the runway. The man in the tower yelled through the radio, "Get off the runway."

The supply planes brought in everything that the men and scientists would need, including booze. Because the three men on Fire Boss were the only ones to meet the

I Was There

planes, they were slipped gallons of Jack Daniels and other spirits for use on off-duty times.

Most men spent their time watching moves, playing cards or riding the shuttle bus that ran from six in the morning until six at night into McMurdo to the recreation center. On his off days, Fuller loved taking pictures, especially of the Emperor Penguins and Weddell Seals. The Emperors are the tallest and heaviest of all of the penguin species. The male and female are similar in plumage and size, reaching forty-eight inches in height and weighing from forty-nine to ninety-nine pounds. As have probably been seen on TV or in the movies, the penguins are black and white like a man's tuxedo and wear a pale-yellow breast. Viewing the Emperor Penguin is one of the reasons adults travel to the Antarctica, to see them first hand.

The Weddell Seals are a large and abundant specie. They were discovered and named in the 1820s during expeditions by James Weddell, the British sealing captain. The seal stays in the water in the winter months to avoid blizzards, with only their head poking through breathing holes in the ice. They are known for their deep dives and can stay underwater for approximately eighty-minutes. The life span of a Weddell Seal is twenty-years. Richard so enjoyed these adventures away from base camp. But, on one certain day while taking a picture of one of the seals it began to chase him. He was thankful that he could outrun it.

————————

At base camp, the men took showers once every ten days as water was extremely limited and heavily

I Was There

monitored. The infrequent bathing was helpful in one respect, keeping the skin from drying out. When a man showered he would hose down, scrub and then quickly hose down again. During the days between showers, the men would scoop up a bucket of snow, bring it indoors and melt it on the stove. A spit-bath to be sure!

The food was excellent according to Fuller. The only food items not available to them were fresh milk and eggs; the cooks used powered eggs and milk. Snow was melted in the men's living quarters when they wanted a cup of instant coffee.

Mailed was delivered every third day. It came via plane from the U.S. to New Zealand and then transferred to a military plane headed for Antarctica. Those flights carrying mail from home were a welcomed sight for the men.

Fuller returned to Rhode Island after seven months and made the rank of Petty Officer Third Class. His new pay hike plus temporary duty pay and also flight pay was pretty substantial income for this Navy man. His duty was with the fire department working twenty-four hours on duty and twenty-four hours off. When asked if he ever slept during that time he said, "Oh yes. The radio operator would wake us if there was an emergency."

It was during that seven month stretch of time that h met Dorcus, a nice young lady who worked for a jewelry company. Fuller's mother lived in Panama City, Florida and she wanted to meet her son's new girlfriend, so he took a three-day leave and they drove down there. During that visit, his mother talked them into getting married, but they could not do so in Florida because the State required blood tests. They didn't have enough time for that, so they drove to Griffin, Georgia where the test was not required.

In September 1968, Fuller returned to Antarctica for another seven month tour of duty, where he worked in the same capacity as before. On a day when he was off duty, Fuller took a trip into McMurdo. Nothing too stirring ever happens in the Antarctic, and when he heard that a tour ship had dropped anchor in the harbor, he wanted to see it. He watched as the passengers were brought ashore by a Guard Cutter, and then asked if he could take a tour of the Cutter. He was given permission, and he thoroughly investigated the ship from bow to stern and port to starboard. To his ultimate surprise, he ran into an old school chum, Bobby Hill, who was stationed aboard the ship. They spent some time reminiscing over the old days.

In March 1969 Fuller returned to the Antarctic for the last time. After his seven months was fulfilled he returned to Rhode Island to work in the fire department. He was discharged that August from the Navy. Months later Fuller wanted to reenlist, but Dorcus would not hear of it. So the two packed up and moved to Panama City, Florida where their son Robert Ray would be born. Fuller had a difficult time finding work there, so he proceeded to Georgia where he worked in a textile mill. He was so dissatisfied. He still had a deep yearning to go back into the Navy.

He fulfilled that desire in 1976 when he re-enlisted into the Navy after a devastating divorce from Dorcus. He again took training at the Great Lakes Training Center, but this time in the machinist school program where he excelled in the top five percent of his class.

I Was There

After schooling he was assigned to the USS Tattnall based in Mayport, Florida just outside Jacksonville. Fuller's job in the engine room was to monitor the operating gauges and to learn the two-hundred different valves needed to run the engines. The guided missile destroyer departed on March 30, 1977 for a seven-month deployment with the 6th Fleet in the Mediterranean Sea. The four-hundred fifty foot ship experienced heavy waves during a bad storm on its way to the big Sea, leaving many on board seasick.

The Tattnall first docked in Lisbon, Portugal where she stayed for ten days. The men were given leave where they experienced the open market places in that beautiful city. Then it was on to Rhoda, Spain and later to Italy. The trip into Athens, Greece was one of Fuller's favorite stops. He loved the food and was excited to see the Coliseum. Other stops took the ship to the French Riviera and on to Alexandria, Egypt, where the men took a bus to Giza to gaze upon Egypt's greatest ancient and amazing attractions, the Great Pyramids and Sphinx. They left Egypt filled with awe as the Tattnall sailed on to Istanbul in the Black Sea.

The ship entered the Sea and the Captain soon noticed a Russian gun ship approaching them. The Tattnal had been cruising at twenty-two knots using only two boilers of its three boilers. He signaled the engine room to bring the third boiler up to the speed of thirty-two knots so that they could chase the Russian ship, which continued for a ways and then anchored. The Tattnal pulled alongside of it. Just then a Russian submarine sailed right up next to the Russian vessel, so the Tattnal's captain hesitated for a moment and then decided to wait and watch as to what would happen next. After three days of playing cat and mouse, the Tattnal's captain determined that his ship should leave the area.

When the ship returned to Mayport, Florida in October 1977, Fuller was tested for the rank of E-5. He passed the written test, but could not pass the medical, so to his great disappointment he was discharged. For the most part, his time in the Navy had given him much pleasure. He had visited and experienced a lot of the world from the frigid Antarctica to the beautiful Mediterranean Sea.

Richard Fuller returned to Panama City where he drove truck for the Sunshine food chain on a route that took him to five surrounding states. Later, he would be employed with the fire department at Tyndall AFB, where he remained until 1984.

While working at Tyndall on swing shift, Richard would stop on his way home from work at Krystal's in Calloway for hamburgers to take back to his apartment. A beautiful young lady by the name of Juli Deannette worked as the night manager and he fell in love with her deep beautiful voice. Every night he ordered ten Krystal burgers, and soon he did not have to place his order, as Juli would have them waiting for him when he walked in each evening. That was the beginning of a budding romance that led to marriage.

When asked what the military service did for him, Richard's response was, "The snot-nosed kid who entered the service matured. It was good for me."

Richard Fuller had a stroke in 2000 which led to other serious complications. Since that time, he has experienced many other medical conditions and finally had to move to

I Was There

the Sims Veterans' Nursing Home for more extensive care than he could receive at home. His beautiful Juli visits him quite often.

◄►

I Was There

War Ends in Vietnam

On January 27, 1973 the United States and North Vietnam signed the Paris Peace Accords. The U.S. agreed to withdraw all military personnel within sixty days. North Vietnam agreed to return *all* American POWs. We know now that that statement would not hold true.

Two million Americans served in Vietnam. Forty-seven thousand were killed. The last of the American military departed that country by March 29, 1973, and only embassy staff remained.

I Was There

Vietnam War Timeline

1858-1884: France invades Vietnam and makes it a colony

Oct 1930: Ho Chi Minh helps found the Indochinese Communist Party

Sep 1940: Japan invades Vietnam

Jan 1950: Vietnam receives military advisors and weapons from China.

Jul 1950: The U.S. pledges $15 million worth of military aid to France to help them fight in Vietnam

Oct 1955: S. Vietnam declares itself the Republic of Vietnam

Dec 1960: The National Liberation Front (NLF – also called the Viet Cong) is established in N. Vietnam

Nov 1963 – S. Vietnamese President is executed during a coup

Aug 1964: N. Vietnamese attack two US destroyers sitting in international waters (the Gulf of Tonkin Incident)

Aug 1964: In response to the Gulf of Tonkin Incident, the US congress passes the Gulf of Tonkin Resolution

Mar 1965: A sustained US serial bombing campaign of N. Vietnam begins (Operation Rolling Thunder)

Mar 1965: First US combat troops arrive in Vietnam

Jan 1968: Tet Offensive – N. Vietnamese joined with Viet Cong to attack one hundred S. Vietnamese cities and towns

I Was There

Timeline continued:

Mar 1968: US soldiers kill hundreds of Vietnamese civilians in Mai Lai

Jul 1968: Gen. Westmoreland replaced by Gen. Abrams

Dec 1968: US troops in Vietnam reaches 540,000

Jul 1969: Pres. Nixon orders the first US troops withdrawn from Vietnam

Sep 1969: Communist revolutionary leader Ho Chi Minh dies at age 79.

Nov 1969: American public learns of the Mai Lai massacre.

Apr 1970: Pres. Nixon announces that US troops will attack enemy locations in Cambodia.

Mar 1972: N. Vietnamese cross the DMZ at the 17th parallel to attack S. Vietnam – known as Easter Offensive

Jan 1973: Paris Peace Accords are signed that provide a cease-fire

Mar 1973: The last US troops are withdrawn from Vietnam

Mar 1975: N. Vietnam launches a massive assault on S. Vietnam

Apr 1975: South Vietnam surrenders to the communists

Jul 1976: Vietnam is unified as a communist country.

◄►

POW∗MIAs

I Was There

The men and women who are prisoners-of-war or missing-in-action are not forgotten by the residents and staff at the Sims Veterans' Home. On tall flag poles adorning the front of the Home the black and white POW/MIA flag flies alongside the American and the State of Florida flags.

Just inside the front lobby, a person's attention is drawn to a small table set with a beautiful place setting of dinnerware. On closer examination visitors and residents alike are awed by the meaning of that one place setting.

The table is adorned with a white lace tablecloth, crystal dinner plate, an upside down crystal goblet, a budvase with a single rose and a candle.

Alongside the tableware a poem has been written to explain the meaning that each item represents.

I Was There

It reads:

This table, set for one is small –symbolizing the frailty of one prisoner alone against his oppressors.

The tablecloth is white, symbolizing the purity of their intentions to respond to their country's call to arms.

The single rose displayed in the vase reminds us of the families and friends of our missing brothers, who kept the faith while awaiting their return.

The red ribbon tied prominently on the vase reminds us of the red ribbons worn on the lapels and brothers who are not among us tonight.

A slice of lemon on the plate reminds us of their bitter fate.

Salt sprinkled on the plate reminds us of the countless fallen tears of families as they wait.

The glass is inverted – they cannot toast with us tonight.

The chair is empty – they are not here.

The candle is reminiscent of the light of hope, which lives in our hearts to light the way home, away from their captors to the open arms of a grateful nation.

Author Unknown

Home Away from Home

The stories that you have read were only a sampling of the many hundreds that could have been told by other residents at the Sims Veterans' Home, ones that would fill a dozen large books. Some residents were reluctant to share their stories, still too painful to relive. Others due to dementia or Alzheimer's were unable to recall the past. They *all* are to be honored.

Bypassing Emily Posts' rule of etiquette for not wearing a hat in the house, the men at Sims are proud to wear their baseball style cap all day long. Their military organization is written across the hat, as well as the medals they've earned are pinned there.

Military organizations in the area are loyal to the men and women at Sims by organizing cookouts, an afternoon at their facility, as well as other events planned for their pleasure. One of the most pleasurable weekly event that takes place each Thursday are dogs on leashes brought to the Veterans' Home to spend some *getting-acquainted* time with the residents. The men and women smile as little children from schools in the area perform for them. Even a karaoke contest between staff and residents has been held, with men and women singing along and tapping their toes to the familiar tunes of yester year.

The Activities Director, Virginia O'Hare, does her best to schedule events for the enjoyment of the residents who make Chester C. Sims Veterans' Nursing Home their home.

I Was There

For further information in regards to the Veterans' Nursing Home feel free to contact them at:

Clifford C. Sims State Veterans' Nursing Home
4419 Tram Road
Springfield, FL 32404-2559
Phone: 850-747-5401
Fax: 850-747-5301

or

Florida Department of Veteran's Affairs website:
www.floridavets.org

◄►

I Was There

About the Author

Author and freelance writer Janet Nicolet resides in Panama City, Florida. She was very young when World War II broke out, but does remember how it was on the home front. She was attending high school during the Korean Conflict, and waited at home with the couple's four children when her husband fought in the Vietnam War.

Ms. Nicolet retired in 2005 at age sixty-nine and wrote her memoir of how God transformed her life after a devastating divorce. She has written an inspirational novel trilogy series titled *Kerri* and also a historical novel. She teaches memoir writing at senior centers in her area.

Books by Janet A. Nicolet:
Non-fiction: A Memoir
"Vintage Years, *A Fulfilling Life after Divorce*" (2007)
Fiction: Inspirational Novels
"Kerri – *An Incredible Journey*" (2008)
"Kerri – *Recaptured Love*" (2009)
"Kerri – *A Sister's Love*" (2010)
"Long Journey Westward" a historical novel (2011)

Books may be ordered from the author's website: **www.myvintageyears.com** or from online bookstores. An eBook format can be ordered on **www.theebooksale.com.**

E-mail comments are invited at
janbythebay21@juno.com.

CPSIA information can be obtained at www.ICGtesting.com
Printed in the USA
236291LV00003B/3/P

9 781849 610964